THE
GROWING
CHURCH

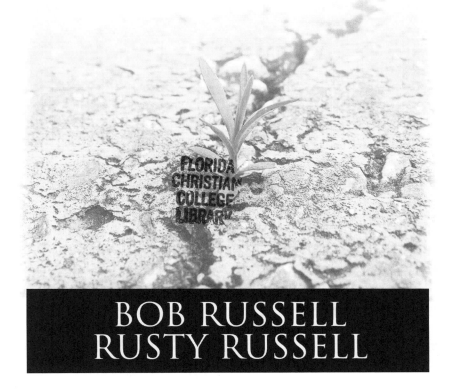

FLORIDA
CHRISTIAN
COLLEGE
LIBRARY

BOB RUSSELL
RUSTY RUSSELL

HEARTSPRING PUBLISHING · JOPLIN, MISSOURI

Copyright © 2007
HeartSpring Publishing ◥◢
www.heartspringpublishing.com
A division of College Press Publishing Co.

Toll-free order line 800-289-3300
On the web at www.collegepress.com

The 3:16 Series (Colossians 3:16)
"Let the word of Christ dwell in you richly . . . ."

Cover design by Brett Lyerla
Interior design by Dan Rees

International Standard Book Number 978-0-89900-928-5

HEARTSPRING'S 3:16 SERIES

The Apostle Paul encouraged Christians in the first century and therefore us today to "**allow the Word of Christ to dwell in us richly**" (Colossians 3:16, *NIV*).

The 3:16 Series is based on this verse in Colossians. The series is designed primarily for small group study and interaction but will also prove fruitful for individual study. Each participant is encouraged to read the chapter before the group's meeting. The interaction questions are designed to be the focal point of your group's discussion time.

Psalm 119:11 says, "*I have hidden Your Word in my heart that I might not sin against You.*" One noteworthy feature of this series is that each study includes a suggested memory verse (a short verse or two from the passage that is being studied). A sheet of these has been included at the back of the book for you to take these verses with you wherever you go and refer to them throughout your day.

The HeartSpring Publishing website will continually be updated with small group ideas and tips to further enhance your study of each New Testament book in the 3:16 series. Be sure to log on to www.heartspringpublishing.com (College Press) frequently!

> "**Let the Word of Christ . . . have the run of the house.**
> **Give it plenty of room in your lives.**"
> (Col. 3:16 *The Message*)

PREVIEWING OUR STUDY OF TITUS

BOB RUSSELL

I was privileged to minister for forty years at a continually growing congregation. Southeast Christian Church grew steadily from a handful of people in the 1960s to over 18,000 members today. In 1999, the year we moved into our newest facility, the average church attendance jumped an incredible 3,000 people! It was wonderful and exciting to see God working in such a dramatic way, but there were also continual challenges to leading that kind of congregation. We were constantly struggling to find the answers to a lot of legitimate questions: How committed are these new members? How will we disciple them? Are we leaving behind our older members? Do people really know what they believe? How do we recruit enough volunteers? How do we utilize everybody's gifts? How can we shepherd such a rapidly increasing number of people?

Though we rejoice whenever a congregation grows rapidly, we must remember that the Great Commission has a two-pronged approach: Make disciples and teach them all things. We are to evangelize and edify. The Kingdom of God is much more than announcing the minimum requirements necessary to get to heaven. It's about transforming people's lives to be like Christ. That is a big challenge because every church is made up of baby Christians who need to be fed, "teenage" Christians who tend to rebel, and immature Christians of all ages. In fact everyone in the church is still a work in progress.

The best place to find answers to questions about how to handle a rapidly growing congregation is the Owner's Manual. The church is the body of Christ; God's Word best explains what the body of Christ should be doing during its growth period. One great place to start in God's Word is the book of Titus.

On one of his missionary journeys, Paul had planted a church on the island of Crete and had appointed Titus as the senior minister of this growing congregation. The island of Crete must have been a dreadful place to try to build a church. Paul says that one of their own writers described the Cretans as "liars, evil brutes, lazy gluttons" (Titus 1:12). But even on this pagan and spiritually hardened island, Paul and Titus had established a growing congregation.

Later Paul wrote Titus a letter giving him instructions on how to order the church during its growth period. A careful study of this letter will remind church leaders of some basic truths regarding what God wants for the body of Christ and will help to ensure that your congregation remains on the right track throughout its growth, regardless of the pressures from the outside world.

TABLE OF CONTENTS

THE GROWING CHURCH

CHAPTER ONE

STAND FIRM IN THE TRUTH

TITUS 1:1-4

After my book *When God Builds a Church* was printed, my publisher scheduled a number of radio and television interviews for me to promote the book. One of the interviews was with our local NPR affiliate in Louisville. I walked into the station expecting to answer another series of softball questions about the book. Instead, the hostess began, "Our guest today is Reverend Bob Russell, minister of Southeast Christian Church in Louisville, Kentucky. It is said this is one of the largest churches in the nation. But some say the church is homophobic, some say it's anti-Semitic, some say it's hostile to women, some say it's a cult. We'll be talking about that when we come back." I gulped! For the next hour and a half I fielded a series of very hostile questions from the hostess and her audience—questions that obviously had been lined up in advance. I've never been so tempted to lie! I decided to keep blaming God instead. I found myself saying, "I'm not the one who decided homosexuality is wrong, that wives should submit to their husbands, or that Jesus is the only way to salvation. We believe the Bible is God's Word, and God's word says . . ." then I would quote the appropriate passages. I'm not sure if it was my fear or the leading of the Holy Spirit that drove me to put the blame back on God's Word, but when the interview was over I was glad that I had relied on the power of God's truth to get me through the difficult questions rather than water down the message.

The church's primary mission is to spread the true gospel of Jesus Christ. But as a church grows, two things happen that cause it to face a strong temptation to dilute the message in order to accommodate the culture. First, the congregation often begins to attract more people of high standing within the community who bring with them not only a lot of prestige, but often a lot of money as well. Nobody wants to offend these influential people.

> **The church's primary mission is to spread the true Gospel of Jesus Christ.**

Second, a growing church is a bigger target for criticism from those who disagree with the church's message. America has rapidly spiraled downward from a Christian culture to a post-Christian culture, and now we are becoming an anti-Christian culture. Today if you dare say that Jesus is the only way to heaven, that homosexuality is a sin, that God created the world, that abortion is the taking of a human life, or that fathers are to lead their homes, then you will be radically opposed by the world. Nobody likes to face a lot of criticism, so we're tempted to avoid the issues or change the message altogether.

Since the temptation to water down the message can be so strong, a growing church must constantly be reminded by the leaders to stand firm in the truth.

The Source of Truth

Paul began his letter,

> Paul, a servant of God and an apostle of Jesus Christ for the faith of God's elect and the knowledge of the truth that leads to godliness—a faith and knowledge resting on the hope of eternal life, which God, who does not lie, promised before the beginning of time, and at his appointed season he brought his word to light through the preaching entrusted to me by the command of God our Savior. . . (Titus 1:1-3).

Paul acknowledged that the source of truth is God himself "who does not lie."

Our country is divided over all kinds of moral issues: the war on terror, pornography, abortion, domestic partnerships, gambling. Nobody knows how to determine right from wrong. Some philosophers say moral judgment should be based on feelings. "If you feel good, then it is right. If you feel bad, then it is wrong." But should we let people do what they feel like doing? Some people feel good only when they're drunk or high.

Others say we should allow the intelligent or famous people of our society to set the standards for morality. But the academic elite and members of the media contradict each other. Do you listen to Sean Hannity or Alan Colmes? Is President Bush right or is Hillary Clinton the one speaking truth?

Many say we should just let majority opinion rule. Have a vote on domestic partner benefits, gambling, and prayer in schools, and let the populace decide. But the Bible says, "There is a way that seems right to a man, but in the end it leads to death" (Prov 14:12). The majority in Germany favored Hitler prior to World War II. The majority of Confederate states in America were in favor of slavery. The majority is seldom right.

> **Many say we should just let majority opinion rule, but the majority is seldom right.**

To end the confusion, most people say we should just let everyone decide for himself or herself what is right and tolerate everybody's beliefs. But if I think it is right for me to drive drunk, should you just tolerate that belief or do you have a duty to persuade me otherwise? The same people who say we should tolerate every belief are supporting advertising campaigns to persuade young people that smoking is bad for you. Does that make sense?

When you are a member of the body of Christ, you have a definite source of truth that does not change. It's not majority opinion or personal feeling; it is the person of Jesus Christ. Jesus told Pilate, "I came into the world . . . to testify to the truth. Everyone on the side of truth listens to me" (John 18:33-37).

But Jesus didn't just claim to be the truth. He proved his claim by coming back from the grave. Anybody can walk around pontificating about God and the Bible and humanity, but Jesus did more than just teach. He said, "For as Jonah was three days and three nights in the belly of a huge fish, so the Son of Man will be three days and three nights in the heart of the earth" (Matt 12:40). When Jesus came back to life, it vindicated his claims and proved his deity. As Paul said, it is Jesus by whom we will be judged: "God . . . commands all people everywhere to repent. For he has set a day when he will judge the world with justice by the man he has appointed. He has given proof of this to all men by raising him from the dead" (Acts 17:30-31).

The Importance of Truth

Truth Gives Meaning to Life

In Titus 1:1 Paul called himself "a servant of God and an apostle of Jesus Christ." Paul knew his life had purpose because he understood the connection between truth and a meaningful life.

Stand Firm in the Truth 1

When a person is interviewed for a job, the interviewer will often ask, "What goals have you set for yourself and how do you plan to achieve them?" Very few people can adequately answer that question. But Paul knew his role in life: he was an apostle, a representative of Jesus Christ, and his goal was to serve the Lord doing whatever God asked him to do. He knew nothing else mattered. When you're not sure what is true, you're not sure what direction your life should take. But once you have fully committed yourself to the truth, you have a purpose in life.

Truth Leads to Godliness

Paul also spoke of "the knowledge of the truth that leads to godliness" (Titus 1:1). God's truth enhances our character. Ignorance of the truth leads to decadence, but knowledge of the truth leads to Godlikeness, integrity, self-discipline, and order.

Following the Indianapolis Colts' first-ever Super Bowl victory, coach Tony Dungee told a national television audience, "All the credit for what has happened to me goes to the Lord." That bold testimony probably makes the media uncomfortable and may even cost him some lucrative endorsements, but he has consistently poured out his own ambitions to bring honor to Christ. He is known as someone who controls his temper, doesn't swear in the locker room, and doesn't yell at his players. Tony Dungee's faith and knowledge of the truth has led to godliness. It has impacted how he responds to adversity and how he treats other people.

> God's truth enhances our character. Ignorance of the truth leads to decadence.

You know about coaches who swear at reporters, throw chairs, abuse referees, and even hit their players. Which of those two types of coaches would you rather have as your neighbor? Which of those two extremes in behavior are going to make a stable society? Jesus said, "The thief comes to steal and destroy; I have come that they may have life, and have it to the full" (John 10:10).

Truth Provides Hope for Eternity

Paul connects the knowledge of truth with "the hope of eternal life" (Titus 1:2). Years ago Steve Brown wrote a book titled, *When Your Rope Breaks*. You've always heard, "When you get to the end of your rope, tie a knot and hold on!" What if you tie a knot and hold on, and then your rope breaks? Maybe your situation is that desperate. Your finances are falling apart, your family is dissolving, or your health is broken. Maybe you're addicted to a habit and you don't know how to break it. That kind of hopeless circumstance sometimes leads to the most extreme behavior. But the truth is that Jesus promises the hope of eternal life even when your rope breaks.

We respect a person who speaks out for God, but I respect Tony Dungee even more because of his consistent testimony in the face of adversity. It's one thing to praise God when things are going well. But Tony Dungee had the same bold testimony several years ago when he got fired from his coaching job in Tampa Bay. And he maintained the same bold faith when his family was devastated by the suicide of his twenty-year-old son, and when they discovered that their youngest son had a rare neurological disease.

Anybody can praise God when things go well. How can Tony Dungee continue to be faithful in the midst of adversity? Because he believes the truth of God's Word when it says, "In all things God works for the good of those who love him, who have been called according to his purpose" (Rom 8:28). Believing the truth brings hope for this life and for eternity.

Truth Deepens Affections

"To Titus, my true son in our common faith: Grace and peace from God the Father and Christ Jesus our Savior" (Titus 1:4) Paul called Titus "my true son." The truth deepens affections. Most relationships are superficial because people put their own needs first. Only in Jesus Christ do we learn to put others ahead of ourselves. Our relationships deepen because we're not just acquaintances. We become brothers, sisters, mothers, fathers, sons, and daughters in the family of God.

Ben Merold had just become the preacher of Eastside Christian Church in Fullerton, California, when he learned that his youngest son had been arrested for peddling drugs and was sent to prison. Ben thought of dropping out of ministry. Some in his church strongly hinted he should.

Tommy Overton, who preached at Huntington Beach, California, heard of Ben's struggle and asked to take him to lunch. Tommy picked up Ben and started driving, making small talk with him for a while. Then Tommy stopped outside a women's prison in Southern California. He said, "Ben, I have a daughter in there. I sometimes drive out here and sit and pray for her. It breaks my heart to know she's in there and I can't help her. Ben, would you like to tell me about your son?"

Ben poured out his heart to Tommy and the two wept together. An instant bond was formed. Tommy helped save Ben's ministry that day, a ministry which has since then reached thousands of people over the span of several decades. The two preachers had a common pain that united them, but many parents have children in prison. They felt comfortable instantly relating deeply to one another because they had a common loyalty to Jesus Christ.

Truth Enhances Our Personality

Following the truth empowers us to give to others "grace and peace from God the Father and Christ Jesus our Savior" (Titus 1:4). Generally speaking, the older people get, the crankier and more worrisome they get. But as Christians get older and become more Christlike, we should become more graceful and peaceful because we know there is still hope.

A missionary to the Kiamichi Mountain Indians in Oklahoma told of driving up to a shanty where an elderly Indian woman sat in a rocking chair on the front porch. He called out to her, "Are you alone, ma'am?"

She cracked a crinkly grin and said, "It's just me and Jesus, son—just me and Jesus."

Though people may sometimes be alone, they don't have to be lonely. They can be full of grace and peace as they get closer to the truth.

The Responsibility of Truth

Knowledge of the truth brings with it a responsibility: We must share it as it is. Paul said that Jesus "brought his word to light through the preaching entrusted to me by the command of God our Savior" (Titus 1:3).

The truth has been entrusted to us and we have been commanded by God to share it. But we must understand the truth is God's message not ours.

If I send a letter by US mail, it's the job of the postal service to deliver that letter intact. They're not allowed to alter it, delete part of it, or add something to it. I don't care how they get it there—by air or truck or foot—but they're supposed to deliver it just as I wrote it.

God has entrusted his message to us. We can use different methods, different music, different buildings, and different kinds of programs, but the message of the truth is not to be altered. It's not ours. Mother Teresa said, "I'm just a little pencil in the hand of God, who is writing a love letter to the world."

Consider some the Scriptures that warn the body of Christ to speak the whole truth:

"What I received I passed on to you as of first importance" (1 Cor 15:3).

Stand Firm in the Truth

"If we or an angel from heaven should preach a gospel other than the one we preached to you, let him be eternally condemned!" (Gal 1:8).

"See that what you have heard from the beginning remains in you. If it does, you also will remain in the Son and in the Father" (1 John 2:24).

In spite of these admonitions, churches are still inclined to dilute the message or add to it in one way or another.

Church leaders need to remember that the most dangerous assaults are always the most subtle. We know to reject Satan's outright attack on the inerrancy of Scripture. When someone openly preaches that the Bible is not God's Word, we rise up in defense. But the devil is always coming up with a craftier scheme. He whispers, "I know the Bible says Jesus is the only way, but that's offensive to people. Leave that for the deeper Bible studies." Or, "How can you take a stand against divorce when so many in your own congregation have been through divorce? Isn't it more important to minister to the brokenhearted and not open old wounds?" Or, "Don't make such strong demands of new Christians. How can they possibly repent of sexual immorality if they've never even known it's wrong? They'll come along in due time."

Satan doesn't have to get the church to reject the truth if he can get us to reduce the truth down to only those parts that are not offensive. He wants us to ignore the offensive parts in favor of tolerance and peace. But Jesus said, "Do not suppose that I have come to bring peace to the earth. I did not come to bring peace, but a sword" (Matt 10:34). Yes, we are to be as loving and merciful as possible, but we must not shy away from the truth. We have been entrusted with a great responsibility. We are to "speak the truth in love" (Eph 4:15).

Another of Satan's tricks is to convince us that we never have to speak the truth at all. If we live the way we're supposed to, he tells us, we should never have to preach the gospel because people will be convinced by our lifestyle. But God's Word says, "How, then, can they call on the one they have not believed in? And how can they believe in the one of whom they have not heard? And how can they hear without someone preaching to them?" (Rom 10:14). Jesus' example is one of both living and preaching the truth. Both are equally important. "If the trumpet does not sound a clear call, who will get ready for battle?" (1 Cor 1:18).

Church leaders are afraid that if we speak the truth, it will seem too demanding and people will be scared away. So we accommodate the message to broaden the appeal. But the sad irony is that a diluted message actually loses its appeal because people are hungry for the real thing. People know down deep that something is drastically wrong with this world and that we need repentance. When the gospel is shared in its

Stand Firm in the Truth 1

purity, it has awesome power. "For the word of God is living and active. Sharper than any double-edged sword, it penetrates even to dividing soul and spirit, joints and marrow; it judges the thoughts and attitudes of the heart" (Heb 4:12).

That's the biggest reason why churches who still preach the Bible are growing while churches that have rejected God's Word are declining in numbers. People are hungry for absolutes. If they come to church knowing that the Bible has those absolutes but they never hear them preached, they go away hungry. As spiritually starving people, they'll begin looking someplace else to be fed.

> "The days are coming," declares the Sovereign LORD, "when I will send a famine through the land—not a famine of food or a thirst for water, but a famine of hearing the words of the LORD. Men will stagger from sea to sea and wander from north to east, searching for the word of the LORD, but they will not find it" (Amos 8:11,12).

It is important that your church stand firm in the truth—that those who teach and preach tell God's truth, the whole truth, and nothing but the truth.

But it's not enough just to tell the truth. Church leaders must live the truth. William Barclay used to say, "A man's message will always be heard in context with his character." If the truth is to have any power through you, there must be an authenticity and transparency about you that makes the truth appealing.

I once stopped to purchase some cookies my wife had asked me to pick up. The woman selling the cookies said, "Are you Bob Russell?"

I said, "Yes, I am."

"You know, I listen to you preach on the radio every Sunday," she said. "And I just want you to know that I really appreciate your messages. The thing I appreciate about your messages is that you are not afraid to stand for the truth the way you see it. Not everybody does that."

I got so distracted admiring how perceptive she was that I left without paying for those cookies! When I got home and realized what I had done, I couldn't call her fast enough. "Mrs. Griffin," I said, "I forgot to pay for those cookies! I'll send you the money right away."

She said, "That's all right. I've heard you preach enough that I knew you'd call back."

I started thinking, *What if I hadn't called back?* If I hadn't righted my wrong, it would have forever negated my messages in her mind. That's

16

‡

C
H
A
P
T
E
R

1 *Stand Firm in the Truth*

why 1 Timothy 4:16 says, "Watch your life and doctrine closely. Persevere in them, because if you do, you will save both yourself and your hearers."

If I hadn't righted my wrong, it would have forever negated my messages in her mind.

If you claim to be standing for the truth, you had better do your best to back up that claim with a consistent lifestyle or the message is nullified. "Stand firm. Let nothing move you. Always give yourselves fully to the work of the Lord, because you know that your labor in the Lord is not in vain" (1 Cor 15:58). 3:16

✝

C
H
A
P
T
E
R

Stand Firm in the Truth   1

Promoting Growth with Truth

1. Which biblical truths do you think are under the greatest assault in our society today?

2. Which truths do you find yourself most tempted to water down?

3. Can you think of a time when accepting a biblical truth changed your life?

4. The Scripture commands us to balance truth and love. Leaning too far to one side leads to dogmatism and legalism. Leaning too far to the other leads to liberalism. To which side do you find yourself tempted to lean? What can you do to guard against the temptation?

5. Every Christian has a responsibility to speak the truth in love. Where do you find yourself having the most opportunity to share God's truth?

6. When we don't speak the truth, it is typically because we lack opportunities or we are afraid to seize the moment. Which is it for you? What could you do to change this?

 Memory Verse Titus 2:1

You must teach what is in accord with sound doctrine.

‡

C
H
A
P
T
E
R

1 *Stand Firm in the Truth*

CHAPTER TWO

CHOOSE YOUR LEADERS CAREFULLY

TITUS 1:5-9

Doug Smith used to tell about a pivotal elders and deacons meeting in a church he once served. The building
committee recommended that the church begin construc-
tion on a much-needed educational wing. During the discussion that followed, two elders were very vocal in opposition.
They insisted the project was too risky and could bankrupt the
church. They gave illustrations of churches that had gone
bankrupt and quoted economists who predicted an upcoming
economic earthquake. They advised against borrowing any
money. Those two leaders persuaded the rest of the church
board to delay the project until more money was available.

Doug says two years later the need was the same. The proposal
was resubmitted and approved. By then the cost of the new building
had almost doubled. After the vote someone asked one of the two former detractors, "Will you drop the extra million in the offering plate
this Sunday to cover the difference?" To his credit the man admitted his
past mistake but added, "Just remember, there were 18 of you who
allowed 2 of us to talk you out of it."

When Paul wrote a letter to Titus about the new congregations that
had been established on the island of Crete, the first thing he did was
to remind Titus of the importance of appointing right leaders. He wrote,
"The reason I left you in Crete was that you might straighten out what
was left unfinished and appoint elders in every town, as I directed you"
(Titus 1:5).

The churches in Crete were growing. They had great potential. But they needed proper leadership. A crucial part of leading a growing con-

> **Two or three people can make a significant difference in the direction of a large body.**

gregation is helping the church recruit and select qualified overseers. Those who have studied leadership dynamics will tell you that two or three people can make a significant difference in the direction of a large body. Every appointment to the board of elders is a crucial decision because those members will have a tremendous influence on the direction of your church.

This passage is specifically about leaders in the church. But let's remember that there is a general implication here for every Christian: choose your leaders wisely. Only Jesus Christ is worthy of our worship, but we all need role models. Hebrews 6:12 reads, "We do not want you to become lazy, but to imitate those who through faith and patience inherit what has been promised." This passage is primarily about church leadership, but it's a good reminder that as we seek to grow in Christ, we should imitate people with these characteristics whether they become overseers or not. Todd Clark, senior minister of Discovery Church, used to be our youth minister at Southeast. He would tell our kids, "Show me your friends and I'll show you your future."

The Definition of Church Leaders

Paul urged Timothy to select "elders in every town." In the New Testament three terms were used interchangeably for the same office: elder, overseer (or bishop),[1] and shepherd (or pastor[2]).[3] Paul expected Titus to wisely select a group of mature spiritual men to lead each congregation.

Notice three things about the description of church leadership that are contrary to popular thought but I believe are scriptural.

The Role Is Gender Specific Not Gender Neutral

Paul says the elder should be the husband of one wife and the overseer of his family. All other biblical examples assume the elders are men of the church. Some men wrongly assume that they are supposed to be in charge because men are superior to women. The Bible says this is not so (Gal 3:28). I don't know why the Scripture designates elder as a male role, but I can speculate as to a couple of possible reasons:

God Has Created Men and Women Differently. There have been some great women leaders throughout history, even in the Bible. The Scripture does not forbid women to hold leadership positions in government or business. Even in the church there are many vital leadership roles a woman can hold. But when women are the elders and pastors of the church, men tend to be completely absent or at best very passively involved. Perhaps it is because the male ego is so weak that if we are not in charge, we just quit. Perhaps it is because women are better at relationships while men are better at charging the hill and accomplishing the task. Perhaps it is because the natural desire in most men is to be protectors and providers. These traits may not be universal to all men or women. But God has created men and women differently, and that may be why God's Word designates elder as a male role.

> When women are the elders and pastors, men tend to be absent or passively involved.

The Husband Is to Be the Head of the House. The Scripture is clear that in a marriage relationship, a wife is to submit to her husband's leadership as she would to Christ Himself (Eph 5:22). Imagine the challenges that would arise in my home if my wife were also my pastor. She has wonderful leadership gifts and would be very capable of being an elder. If I were a member in her congregation, where would the authority of the church end and the authority of the home begin? If a Christian marriage is supposed to be one where the husband is the head, then it makes sense that in Christian churches, men—primarily husbands—take the leadership roles so that there is not a contradiction.

These are not perfect answers, but they may be some of the reasons for designating male leadership in the church. Whatever the conclusions, we need to make sure to let the Scriptures be our guide no matter what popular opinion may be.

The Church Is a Christocracy Not a Democracy

This is the second truth that goes against popular thought. Americans think everything should be determined by popular vote. But Paul didn't tell Titus to hold a congregational meeting and take a vote whenever he needed to make a decision. He said, "Titus, appoint elders in each town." The Bible does not dictate what the nominating process should be, but once the elders are chosen, they need to lead. We shouldn't subject every decision to a popular vote.

There Is a Plurality of Elders Not a Lone Pastor

God in his wisdom did not establish a pastor-ruled church. He instructed that there be several elders or pastors leading the congregation together. It is appropriate for one of the elders to do most of the preaching and teaching and receive a salary (1 Tim 5:17), but he is just one of several overseers or pastors.

When I was the senior minister of Southeast Christian Church, I was considered one of more than a dozen elders, the rest of whom were volunteers. I worked hard to maintain a good spirit of cooperation with the elders. I believe our unity was one of the reasons God blessed our congregation so dramatically. Our elders acknowledged my gifts and were supportive of my leadership, but I acknowledged their authority over me and tried to be submissive. They also knew my weaknesses and worked to help me overcome them. They were never rubber stamps. They would ask tough questions, they made the staff and me accountable for every dime we spent, and they would often register objections when they disagreed with the way things were handled. On the opposite end of the spectrum, some of them were also great visionaries who would bring to the table aggressive ideas for expanding God's kingdom. That kind of diverse but unified leadership is needed for the church to be strong.

> Diverse but unified leadership is needed for the church to be strong.

Qualifications of Church Leaders

In Titus 1:6-9 Paul underscores some of the most important qualifications for leadership in the church. Twice in this passage Paul says an elder must be *blameless* (Titus 1:6). I don't know of any person who is completely blameless. I think Paul means, *not subject to a damaging accusation that would embarrass the church.* An elder needs to be someone who is living a sincere and open life, free from legitimate accusations.

His Family Life

"An elder must be blameless, the husband of but one wife, a man whose children believe and are not open to the charge of being wild and disobedient" (Titus 1:6).

He is to be a godly husband. Paul says an elder must be the "husband of but one wife" (Titus 1:6). Some have taken that to mean he is never to have been divorced and remarried. But to disqualify someone for something he may have had no control over and may have happened years before would be inconsistent with the way we apply the other qualifications. An elder must also "not be given to drunkenness," but we don't disqualify someone who got drunk twenty years earlier as a young man. Divorce is a very serious matter that should not be taken lightly, but it doesn't seem to be Paul's intention to automatically disqualify someone from eldership if he has a divorce in his past.

Most conservative scholars say the phrase means literally "a one-woman man." Polygamy was not widely practiced in Paul's day, but there were religious leaders who taught that it was acceptable and political leaders who practiced it. Paul makes it clear that elders are not to be polygamous. Just as important, an elder should be a "one-woman man" in

> An elder should be a "one-woman man" in his heart.

his heart. He should have a solid commitment to his wife, not be a womanizer, and have a reputation for being sexually pure.

He is to be a godly father. Paul also says an elder is to be "a man whose children believe and are not open to the charge of being wild and disobedient" (Titus 1:6). You can tell a lot about a man by observing his family. If his children are out of control and rebellious, or if they never come to church, or if he attends the PTA meeting under an assumed name because his kids have such a bad reputation at school, don't follow him as a leader. If he isn't leading his family well, he's not ready to lead in the church.

However, we need to be realistic. Everybody's children disobey on occasion. Billy Graham's son Franklin went through a period of outright rebellion and turned his back on Christianity. Since then Franklin has turned back to Christ and has developed an outstanding ministry of his own. When a child grows up and leaves home, his parents no longer have control and should not be held accountable for the child's choices. Paul's point is for us to examine a person's spiritual maturity and leadership ability by studying his leadership in the home. Did his children respect him and desire to follow his faith while they were under his roof?

His Social Life

"Since an overseer is entrusted with God's work, he must be blameless—not overbearing, not quick-tempered, not given to drunkenness, not violent, not pursuing dishonest gain. Rather he must be hospitable. . ." (Titus 1:7-8a).

How a person relates to others outside his family and how he appears in public also tell a lot about whether he is qualified to be an elder.

He should not be overbearing. The King James translates the phrase "not self-willed." The elder is to be a humble servant-leader like Jesus his Lord, not domineering and intimidating like leaders of the world.

Have you ever gone on a trip with a domineering person? You have to eat at his choice of restaurants, take his route, follow his schedule. You let him lead because you're afraid of offending him or incurring his wrath. Don't imitate a person who manipulates people like that. Don't follow him. Inevitably he will take you where you don't want to go and make you miserable. And certainly don't choose such a person as an elder in your congregation.

He should be slow to anger. Paul says an elder should not be "quick tempered." If a man has a volatile temper, not only might he do something in public that embarrasses the church, but you can also predict that he'll make rash, angry decisions and be divisive in meetings.

He should be sober. The next qualification of an elder is, "not given to drunkenness." It is impossible to calculate the destruction to our society that has been caused by drunkenness. Talk to a police officer, and he will tell you that nearly every arrest, fatal accident, violent crime, and domestic dispute involves alcohol.

Because of our example and because of the devastating consequences of alcohol consumption in our society, I think it is wise for a Christian—and especially a church leader—to be a total abstainer. I wish I could quote a Scripture verse that said, "You shall not drink." I believe it is wise, but it is not a direct command of Scripture. I have never met a person who became a teetotaler and later regretted it, but I have met many people who regretted their past drinking and became teetotalers. The Bible says, "Do not get drunk on wine, which leads to debauchery. Instead, be filled with the Spirit" (Eph 5:18). I'm convinced that the more you are filled with God's Spirit, the less you need alcohol. The church leader should set an example in this area. At Southeast Christian Church we decided to ask our elders and deacons to be total abstainers so that they could avoid even the appearance that they were given to drunkenness.

> I have never met a person who became a teetotaler and later regretted it, but many who regret previous drinking.

He is not to be violent. The King James says, "Not a striker." It's surely no accident that Paul strung together these three characteristics, ". . . not quick-tempered, not given to drunkenness, not violent. . . ." A person who is slow to anger and stays away from alcohol is much less likely to lash out at someone, curse someone, or hit someone when situations are stressful. A man who does such things should not be an elder.

He should not be pursuing dishonest gain. If a man cheats other people in the business world or has an immoral occupation, he should not be leading in the church.

He must be hospitable. The Greek word for hospitable literally means "a lover of guests." The *Living Bible* paraphrases the phrase, "must enjoy having guests in their homes." An elder's home should be a safe and peaceful place where fellowship and deeper relationships occur naturally.

His Personal Life

". . . one who loves what is good, who is self-controlled, upright, holy and disciplined" (Titus 1:8). An elder needs to be a person of deep personal integrity. People don't expect their leaders to be perfect, but they do expect them to be authentic, honest, and pure. Though he doesn't have to be a model of perfection, he should be a model of growth and spiritual maturity. Though it is impossible to know what happens in a person's quiet moments, the evidence should suggest that he is an even deeper person in private than he appears to be in public.

> An elder needs to have deep personal integrity.

Convictions of Church Leaders

"He must hold firmly to the trustworthy message as it has been taught, so that he can encourage others by sound doctrine and refute those who oppose it" (Titus 1:9). A church will remain doctrinally sound if the church leaders remain doctrinally sound, so it is important that the board of elders and the congregation monitor the lifestyle and beliefs of each elder, teacher, and staff member. Unlike Jesus Christ, who is the same yesterday, today, and forever, people change. A cult leader typically starts off with fairly normal beliefs but changes course over time. People blindly follow him or her because they've learned to trust and admire the person. We need to be like the Bereans in Acts 17:11 who "examined the Scriptures every day to see if what Paul said was true."

Paul says an elder who holds to the truth can then "encourage others by sound doctrine." We often think of doctrine as being boring and discouraging, but in a world where the foundations are crumbling, people are encouraged when a leader says, "Here is exactly where we stand. This is what the Bible says, so we will stand on that. It may not be popular, but it's right." People respect the leader and are refreshed by that message because they know he is standing on a solid foundation.

One of the toughest jobs of an elder is to "refute those who oppose" the sound doctrine. A shepherd doesn't just feed and love the sheep;

sometimes he must protect them against the wolves. At times it is essential for the leader to confront error. It should be done as lovingly as possible, but repeatedly in Scripture the elder is told to rebuke and refute when necessary.

Most of us find confrontation distasteful. In fact if you don't find it distasteful there's probably something wrong with your character! When false doctrine arises, it's tempting to compromise on our principles in order to maintain harmony. I've seen leaders take a stand against false teaching and then face criticism from other Christians because they are rocking the boat. When the leader does have the courage to confront error, it's important that the congregation respect him, trust his judgment, and support his courageous stand.

If, for example, the elders decide a certain Bible study is full of false doctrine, follow their advice and stay away from the study. Remember Hebrews 13:17, which reads, "Obey your leaders and submit to their authority. They keep watch over you as men who must give an account. Obey them so that their work will be a joy, not a burden, for that would be of no advantage to you."

When Paul was preaching on the island of Cyprus in Paphos, they converted the mayor. But the mayor's sidekick Elymas, a sorcerer, bitterly opposed Paul. He tried to convince the mayor to change his beliefs. What did Paul do about this man's false teaching?

> Paul, filled with the Holy Spirit, looked straight at Elymas and said, "You are a child of the devil and an enemy of everything that is right! You are full of all kinds of deceit and trickery. Will you never stop perverting the right ways of the Lord? Now the hand of the Lord is against you. You are going to be blind, and for a time you will be unable to see the light of the sun" (Acts 13:9-11).

Immediately Elymas went blind. If you had been there when Paul refuted Elymas, would you have come to the sorcerer's defense? "Paul, that's not very loving! This poor individual!" The Bible says Paul was filled with the Holy Spirit. The man needed to be rebuked and stopped so that the true Gospel could continue to spread.

It is important that we choose leaders wisely, because when difficulty comes and Satan mounts a frontal attack, our leaders must be men who understand their role. They must be men of personal character who stand strong for truth. Only then can the church continue to be distinctive as the people of God. ⬚

[1] Bishop is a transliteration of the Greek word *episkopos*, meaning we simply took the Greek word, transposed the letters into English and made it into an English word without translating its meaning. Overseer is an accurate translation of the meaning of the word.

[2] The Latin word *pastor* means "shepherd."

[3] See Acts 20:17ff where all three terms—elder, shepherd, overseer—are used to describe the Ephesian elders.

Promoting Growth through Leaders

1. What are the most important qualifications of an elder? Is it more important that they *don't* do the things Paul says not to do, or that they *do* the things Paul says they should do?

2. Think of the person you know who exhibits these traits the best. Do you follow that person? What impact has he or she had on your life? The community? The church?

3. The most difficult challenge in choosing leaders is that no human leader is perfect. Consider the traits on a scale of 1-10. If ten is equal to Jesus, how high on the scale must a person be before he is qualified to be an elder? If your answer differs from most in your church, what problems could that cause? How should those problems be solved?

4. The way to take this issue seriously without dividing the church is for the body of Christ to put egos aside and seek the Holy Spirit's guidance. How could your church do that?

5. Think of the five people in your life who have the most influence on you. How many of them would meet the spiritual qualifications of this passage? If your greatest influencers are not leading you spiritually, what should you do about it? Is this an important enough issue to merit radical changes in your life?

Memory Verse
Titus 1:8-9

Rather he must be hospitable, one who loves what is good, who is self-controlled, upright, holy and disciplined. He must hold firmly to the trustworthy message as it has been taught, so that he can encourage others by sound doctrine and refute those who oppose it.

CHAPTER THREE

GUARD AGAINST LEGALISM

TITUS 1:10-16

P rior to World War II France developed a line of defense along its eastern border called the Maginot Line. It was a massive buildup of guns, ammunition, and fortification. France was determined to thwart the inevitable invasion of Germany. But when Hitler's attack came, the Maginot Line was unsuccessful in stopping the German blitzkrieg. The enemy, for the most part, did not break through the line. Instead, in March of 1940, Hitler's forces came *around* the Maginot Line and invaded through the Netherlands, Belgium, and Luxembourg. France fell within two months because the enemy chose a different attack point than the one they were expecting.

Today most Bible-believing churches are digging in against liberalism, and rightly so. Basic moral values are under attack and the integrity of the Bible is being questioned. We need to stand firm in the faith because the faith that was "once for all entrusted to the saints" (Jude 3) is the only faith that promises eternal life. But Satan is a cunning adversary who will go to any length to destroy the church. While we dig our trenches to resist a frontal assault from liberalism, we need to guard against legalism attacking from the other side.

Liberalism may threaten the church's sense of purpose, but the blitzkrieg of legalism will destroy the morale of the Lord's army. "The letter kills, but the Spirit gives life" (2 Cor 3:6). In this passage, Paul gives a strict warning against some legalists, reminding us that we need to guard against this sneak attack in the church.

The Problem of Legalism

"For there are many rebellious people, mere talkers and deceivers, especially those of the circumcision group. They must be silenced, because they are ruining whole households by teaching things they ought not to teach—and that for the sake of dishonest gain" (Titus 1:10-11). The dictionary defines legalism as "a strict or excessive conformity to a law or moral code for the purpose of self-exaltation." Christianity is different from every other religion in the world because

> **Christianity is based not on a set of rules but on the worship of a person.**

it is based not on a set of rules but on the worship of a person—Jesus Christ. Paul wrote to the Romans, "Therefore, there is now no condemnation for those who are in Christ Jesus, because through Christ Jesus the law of the Spirit of life set me free from the law of sin and death" (Rom 8:1-2). By accepting this new rule of salvation through the free gift of God's grace, we are set free from the old laws.

But legalists still believe that God's favor will depend on our exact obedience to rules. They love a list of do's and don'ts, and they judge others by their arbitrary code.

Jesus Encountered Legalists

Jesus encountered both liberals and legalists. The Sadducees were the liberals of the day, denying much of the Old Testament, refusing to believe in life after death or miracles. But the Pharisees were the legalists. Jesus' harshest words were reserved for them because they were the most demanding, insensitive, and selfish people he encountered.

To the Pharisees, the Old Testament wasn't explicit enough. They had their special commentary—the Talmud—where they elaborated on what the Old Testament really meant. For example, the Old Testament said they were to remember the Sabbath day and keep it holy, not doing any work on that day. But what constituted work? The Talmud described in detail what you could or couldn't do on the Sabbath. You couldn't walk more than seven-tenths of a mile. If a hen laid an egg on the Sabbath, you couldn't eat it because the hen was working on the Sabbath. If a man had a sore throat, he couldn't take anything for it because that would be practicing medicine.

The Pharisees hated Jesus because he didn't adhere to their strict code. "Why aren't you fasting as we do?" they would ask. "Why are you healing people on the Sabbath?" "Why are you eating with sinners and publicans?"

In Matthew 23 Jesus responded to the Pharisees, describing their rules as heavy loads that they put on men's shoulders, calling them blind guides and hypocrites who were clean on the outside but full of greed and self-indulgence on the inside. At the end of his speech Jesus indicated how serious legalism is, saying to the Pharisees, "You snakes! You brood of vipers! How will you escape being condemned to hell?" (Matt 23:33).

Paul Encountered Legalists

Most of the book of Galatians was written to defend against a legalistic group who believed you must become a Jew before you could become a Christian. These "Judaizers" demanded that Gentiles become circumcised Jews before becoming Christians, and that Jewish Christians should continue to observe the Sabbath laws, dietary laws, and religious customs of the Jews. Titus was having problems with these same people, whom Paul referred to as "those of the circumcision group" (Titus 1:10). We'll discuss below how Paul demanded that Titus deal with these legalists.

We Encounter Legalists

Not only did Jesus and Paul encounter legalists, we still face them today.

Legalists create church policies. A church in Tennessee established a policy that all men in their church had to keep their hair short because the Bible says that nature tells you a man shouldn't wear long hair. Not only did the policy describe exactly what "short hair" meant but what would happen if someone didn't comply: "Any man whose hair goes beyond his collar will not be welcomed within ten feet of the communion table."

> Jesus and Paul encountered legalists and so do we.

When women first started wearing pants, churches established dress codes for women that said, "Women are not to come to church in slacks." Never mind that the slacks were often more modest than the skirts!

For years only the Latin translation of the Greek New Testament was allowed in churches, even if only the priest understood Latin. Similarly, some churches today have a rule that the preacher can use no other translation in the pulpit but the King James Version.

A few years ago when men first started wearing facial hair again, many churches set up rules against facial hair because they said it was a sign of rebellion. I can only imagine how rebellious it must have seemed to past cultures when men first started shaving their beards!

Well-meaning Christians can attempt to enforce all kinds of rules

> **Well-meaning Christians can attempt to enforce all kinds of rules on the church.**

on the church: every service must end with an invitation; no tapes or records should be sold in the vestibule of the church; no taped background music or drums will be used on Sunday morning; no speaker from an outside denomination will be allowed to share this pulpit; no divorced person will be married in this church; no musical instrument will be used in worship; people must only be baptized on Sunday mornings during church.

Legalists demand compliance to certain lifestyle rules. Legalists may demand that you don't go to movies, don't listen to certain styles of music, don't dance, don't buy a lottery ticket, or don't drink caffeine. Others may say it's wrong to eat meat or drive an SUV. Legalists fail to distinguish between their strong opinions and the Word of God, placing rules where God did not intend rules to be. Their rules become the standard by which they gauge the spirituality of themselves and others.

I went to college with a young man who came from an ultraconservative church. He was so legalistic he thought it was wrong to drink a cup of coffee because it had caffeine in it. When someone pointed out that his favorite soft drink had caffeine, he was devastated. He nearly drove himself crazy trying to keep his own rules, afraid he would do something wrong. Two things matured him: First, he got married, which forced him to recognize that he wasn't perfect. Secondly, he began ministering in a church where he truly loved the people, and that concern for others mellowed his spirit. Years later a mutual friend told me he actually saw him laughing at himself.

There's not much joy in the life of a legalist because if you believe you will earn God's favor by obeying the rules, you'll always be frustrated. There's not much authenticity either, because a legalist is constantly tempted to cover up who he really is lest people find out he's not really that good.

The Causes of Legalism

Selfishness

One reason people are motivated to be so rigid is their innate selfishness. Paul tells Titus they're motivated by "dishonest gain" (Titus 1:11). A televangelist may take a dogmatic stance not because he believes it, but because that's what will motivate a segment of his audience to get angry at the world and give money to his ministry. Sometimes a dogmatic position makes a selfish person feel secure or superior, and sometimes the dogmatist is just plain greedy or power hungry.

A Poorly Trained Conscience

The conscience is far from a perfect guide. The Bible talks about a *seared* conscience (1 Tim 4:2), describing a person who feels no guilt when he should. But the legalist often has what the Bible calls a *weak* conscience (1 Cor 8:10-12), which means he truly feels guilty if he violated his legalistic rules. People who have weak consciences may feel guilty if they eat sweets, work on Sunday, listen to a certain type of music, wear shorts, or have fun in any fashion. Paul says, ". . . their minds and their consciences are corrupted" (Titus 1:15).

When we first started Saturday night worship services, we encountered a lot of legalists. Some of our members would attend on Saturday night then feel guilty not going on Sunday morning. If they left the house, they'd put a tie on so people would think they had been to church! Even if intellectually you believe you have a certain freedom, it's easy to gravitate back to what your spiritual mentor or your parents told you, and those voices in your conscience make you feel guilty.

A Dogmatic Interpretation

Like the Pharisees and Judaizers, people today sometimes develop a legalistic spirit because of their dogmatic interpretation of certain passages of Scripture. Most of the Bible is not difficult to understand. But some passages are challenging to apply to different cultures. The Bible is timeless truth, but the application of biblical principles may change. For example, in 1 Timothy 2:9 Paul says, "I also want women to dress modestly, with decency and propriety, not with braided hair or gold or pearls or expensive clothes." The principle is clear and timeless: women should dress modestly, with decency and propriety. But the application—not braiding your hair or wearing gold or pearls—shouldn't be applied legalistically.

> Some passages are challenging to apply to different cultures.

I heard one professor give this illustration: Imagine that you are on an island in the Pacific Ocean where pearls are in abundance. All the women on the island wear dresses made of pearls. Then one day a box floats onto the coast of the island from a vessel that had been shipwrecked some time ago. In the box are a few old coats with brass buttons on them. Some of the women begin cutting off the buttons and sewing them onto their pearl dresses. The women who have the brass buttons on their pearl dresses begin to act superior to those who have no brass buttons. If Paul were to write to that island about dressing with decency and propriety, would he tell them not to wear pearls? No, he would tell them to stop putting brass buttons on their dresses. To apply a biblical principle legalistically in a different culture can force us to entirely miss the intended message.

There is, however, a balance. We shouldn't go to the opposite extreme and casually dismiss Scriptures as being cultural or figurative. Suppose your boss says he's leaving for a week and gives you a list of ten things he wants you to do while he's gone. The last item on the list says, "I want you to work your fingers to the bone." You don't get legalistic about item number ten because you know that's figurative. He doesn't expect to come back and see skin worn off your fingers. But just because one statement is figurative doesn't mean you can dismiss the other nine items and say, "I'm not going to do any of it because he was obviously speaking figuratively." If you dismiss the whole list, you'll be looking for a new job!

We should respect God's Word as true and timeless, then be sensitive to the leading of the Holy Spirit and common sense when studying certain difficult Scriptures. Remember that the principles of God's Word are timeless, but the proper application of those principles may vary in different cultures.

> **The principles of God's Word are timeless, but proper application may vary with culture.**

The Characteristics of Legalism

Since they pose a serious danger to the church, Paul describes the legalists in very unflattering terms.

Rebellion

Paul says they are "rebellious people." Legalists rebel against the concept of grace, the very heart of the gospel.

Hypocrisy

"They are mere talkers," says Paul. Legalists are very outspoken against sin, but they don't back up their talk with their lifestyle. One televangelist was always hounding about immorality and pornography, then the media disclosed he was meeting prostitutes in a motel. Watch out for the crusader, for the Christian who is always riding a hobby horse. Often the very sin with which he is obsessed is the one he is committing.

Deception

Paul told Titus, "To the pure, all things are pure, but to those who are corrupted and do not believe, nothing is pure" (Titus 1:15). Paul says they are deceivers (1:10). On the surface they appear spiritual but often are not.

Not only is the legalist deceptive, the rules themselves are deceiving. Legalistic rules promise to lead to a life of purity when often the opposite occurs. Rules don't restrain disobedience, they stimulate it. Have you ever gone by a bench that says, "WET PAINT DON'T TOUCH"? What do you want to do? You would have walked by without paying any attention to that bench, but because it says don't touch, you want to touch it! "For when we were controlled by the sinful nature, the sinful passions aroused by the law were at work in our bodies, so that we bore fruit for death" (Rom 7:5). The law sometimes arouses sinful passions.

> Rules don't restrain disobedience, they stimulate it.

One Sunday I told my congregation about a woman in a church nearby who takes her keys out of her pocket and starts rattling them when she thinks it's time for the preacher to quit. It wasn't three minutes later that I heard people in my congregation rattling their keys! They would never have thought about doing that if I hadn't mentioned it!

A preacher on the west coast once announced he had listed every possible sin. The list contained 354 sins. He got letters from all over the country asking for the list! Paul wrote to the Colossians,

> Since you died with Christ to the basic principles of this world, why, as though you still belonged to it, do you submit to its rules: "Do not handle! Do not taste! Do not touch!"? These are all destined to perish with use, because they are based on human commands and teachings. Such regulations indeed have an appearance of wisdom, with their self-imposed worship, their false humility and their harsh treatment of the body, but they lack any value in restraining sensual indulgence (Col 2:20-23).

I went to camp years ago with a legalistic dean who started out the week with a long list of rules for the high school students. One rule stated no girl could wear shorts more than six inches above the knee. That was all the campers talked about all week long! The girls talked about whether one another's shorts were too short. The boys volunteered to measure. It was a bad week.

I went to another week where the dean had more wisdom and better leadership. He said, "We want everybody to dress modestly. If you wear something I think is immodest, I will tell you and have you go change immediately." On a couple of occasions, he did privately have that difficult conversation. The campers respected that dean and didn't give nearly as much attention to their attire that week. Instead they focused more of their attention on the essentials.

Legalism is deceptive. It looks good. "We're going to play by the rules." But it lacks value in restraining evil.

Divisiveness

Paul said, "They are ruining whole households by teaching things they ought not to teach" (Titus 1:11). Maybe you know what it's like to have tension in your home because your parents don't like the church you have joined. Maybe you have Christian friends or siblings who wonder about your salvation because you use instruments when you worship or because you don't observe the Lenten season. I know of a church that changed their minds about giving thousands of dollars to a church plant because the minister of the new church called himself a pastor in the church paper. They believed the proper term should have been *evangelist* instead of pastor, so they dropped their support. Imagine the spirit of division that created.

The Cure for Legalism

Confront the Legalist

Paul was emphatic that a legalist must be confronted quickly. "They must be silenced," he said, "because they are ruining whole households by teaching things they ought not to teach" (Titus 1:11). Don't be naïve about legalism. Be perceptive enough to recognize that it presents a serious threat to the spirit of your family and your church. When legalism surfaces, confront it. "Rebuke them sharply," Paul said (Titus 1:12).

When legalism surfaces, confront it.

Disregard the Concerns of a Legalist

Paul wanted the church to "pay no attention to Jewish myths or to the commands of those who reject the truth" (Titus 1:14). Not all criticism should be ignored because sometimes it can be valid. But when a legalist complains because you're not obeying his list of rules, disregard it. It is tempting to cater to the legalist to keep the peace. Don't do that or you will worry yourself and those around you to death. "To the pure, all things are pure" (Titus 1:15). Rather than trying to defend every action, emphasizing our freedom in Christ may be the most effective way to deal with legalism. Let others see a joy and freedom in your life. "Where the Spirit of the Lord is, there is freedom" (2 Cor 3:17).

On the other hand, don't flaunt your freedom. The Bible also commands us not to do that which would cause someone with a weak conscience to stumble (1 Cor 8:10). Consider those who are following your example and be wise. You may think you have the freedom to drink a glass of wine with your meal, and you are right. But if your actions cause a young person or an immature Christian to begin a habit he can't control, you have acted foolishly. In a similar discussion, regarding eating meat that had been sacrificed to idols, Paul concluded,

> So this weak brother, for whom Christ died, is destroyed by your knowledge. When you sin against your brothers in this way and wound their weak conscience, you sin against Christ. Therefore, if what I eat causes my brother to fall into sin, I will never eat meat again, so that I will not cause him to fall (1 Cor 8:11-13).

When someone under your influence could be led down a dangerous path by your actions, don't flaunt your freedom. But when someone who should know better demands that you follow his legalistic rules, "pay no attention" to his commands.

Seek Unity

Have you ever noticed how we put people in camps? Someone who drives faster than you is a maniac, but everybody who drives slower than you is an idiot. You are the only one in the world who drives the right speed! We do the same thing in the church, labeling people legalists or liberals. The New Testament gives us lots of freedom and very few rules, but God does command

Keep the balance.

us to do our part to keep the church unified: "Make every effort to keep the unity of the Spirit through the bond of peace" (Eph 4:3). Keep the balance, remembering, "In doctrine unity, in opinion liberty, in all things love." Stand firm in the truth of the Bible, but be flexible in matters of opinion.

Develop a Proper Concept of God

Do you envision God as a tyrant ready to strike you every time you disobey? Or is God a loving Father, anxious to forgive and restore you? Your concept of God will determine whether you live in fear or freedom.

Louis Hines wrote an essay about the first time he found out what his father was really like. As a little boy he admired his father but feared him too. One day he was sitting beside his dad in church and began to nod off during the sermon. Out of the corner of his eye he saw his dad's arm move toward him. He was afraid he would be disciplined for falling asleep in church. But his dad put his arm around Louis and drew him to himself. When Louis looked up, his dad winked at him. Louis nestled in his dad's arm and went to sleep.

Jesus said, when you pray, say, "Our Father in heaven. . ." (Matt 6:9). Jesus said, "Do not let your hearts be troubled . . . In my Father's house are many rooms. . ." (John 14:1,2). Jesus said that God is like a father who runs to welcome home a wayward son and smothers the son's repentant speech against his shoulder (Luke 15:11-32).

Allow God to put his loving arm around you and forgive and comfort you. "Where the Spirit of the Lord is, there is freedom" (2 Cor 3:17). He offers you freedom from guilt and sin and death, and freedom from the law. 3:16

  Guard against Legalism

Promoting Growth
While Avoiding Legalism

1. It's tempting to put people in camps, judging everyone else as too legalistic or too liberal. Consider your own life. In what areas have you personally battled a legalistic attitude? Have you been guilty of judging others who disagreed with you? Do you see your legalism and self righteousness as sin? Are you willing to repent?

2. What does Paul mean when he says, "To the pure, all things are pure" (Titus 1:15)?

3. Why was Jesus so harsh toward the Pharisees?

4. It's not wrong to have strong opinions, but it is wrong to be divisive (Titus 3:10). Can Christians have healthy discussions about certain difficult Scriptures and yet maintain their unity? If so, how can they do so? When should you speak up, and when should you keep your beliefs about controversial subjects to yourself (Rom 14:22)?

5. Perhaps the most disregarded command of the New Testament is the command for God's people to be unified. What steps could you take to unify the body of Christ?

To the pure, all things are pure, but to those who are corrupted and do not believe, nothing is pure. In fact, both their minds and consciences are corrupted.

CHAPTER FOUR

SET THE EXAMPLE

TITUS 2:1-3

One of General Patton's soldiers told about a time when they were marching across Europe and came to a swollen river. The soldiers began to complain that there was no way they could cross the raging current carrying their backpacks. Patton said nothing. He strapped on his backpack, waded into the river, swam to the other side, turned around and swam back to his men. Once he was again on their shore, he barked, "Follow me," and headed back into the water. Without protest, everyone in the battalion followed him across to the other side.

One of our greatest needs in the church today is godly mentors. We're inspired more by example than by instruction, but many of our heroes are seriously deficient in the character department. Athletes are into gambling and illegal steroids. Politicians and entertainers are into egotism or dishonest gain. Religious leaders are often disclosed as hypocritical or self-centered. If the church is going to be strong in a pagan culture, it needs some mature Christians who inspire people by their walk with God.

Teachers

Paul is speaking to Titus specifically, but his words apply to all teachers when he says, "You must teach what is in accord with sound doctrine" (Titus 2:1). Anyone who is a school teacher, youth sponsor, small group leader, professor, or in any other field of education should pay attention to Paul's instructions. James wrote, "Not many of you should presume to be teachers, my brothers, because you know that we who teach will be judged more strictly" (Jas 3:1).

When you first accept a teaching position, there is some glamour. It's exciting to think that you will affect people's lives. In the early days your students compliment you and encourage you. But it's not long before the glitter wears off. After a while you discover teaching is hard work and people don't compliment you as much. They may even criticize you or take you for granted.

Teaching is hard work.

One day it hits you: *This is a serious responsibility. This is a long-term commitment. If I don't make a change, I'll be doing this the rest of my life!* But then on a better day you realize, *A few people are actually listening to what I say and it's making a difference in their lives!*

The Bible says God has equipped some people to become pastors and teachers. I think more people are called to teach than answer the call. God would not bless the church with an abundance of children without equipping many to lead them. If you're a teacher, you can resonate with what Paul wrote when he said, "I am compelled to preach. Woe to me if I do not preach the gospel!" (1 Cor 9:16).

We teach because we have to. We teach because we care about people. It may not be the most glamorous position, but it is one of the most rewarding. If the gospel really saves people, if Christ really changes lives, then we can't help but share what we know, even if it's risky. "For Christ's love compels us, because we are convinced that one died for all. . ." (2 Cor 5:14).

A teacher has a dual responsibility:

Teach Accurately

Paul says, "Teach what is in accord with sound doctrine" (Titus 2:1). If you begin to alter the teachings of the Bible, you are usurping the authority of God and endangering the eternal destiny of your students.

Teachers want to be considered intellectual, so they are often tempted to flirt with the latest philosophies and criticisms of the Bible. Don't allow your students to get the impression that you are more interested in controversies and being faddish than in teaching the truth (1 Tim 1:3,4). We're dealing with life-and-death matters, with heaven and hell. We can't be casual with our teaching as if it doesn't matter. The Bible instructs us to be diligent and faithful in our study of the Word. Paul told Timothy, "Do your best to present yourself to God as one approved, a workman who does not need to be ashamed and who correctly handles the word of truth" (2 Tim 2:2).

Live It Faithfully

In everything set them an example by doing what is good. In your teaching show integrity, seriousness and soundness of speech that cannot be condemned, so that those who oppose you may be ashamed because they have nothing bad to say about us (Titus 2:7,8).

If you teach the truth, some people will oppose you. They don't want to hear that they are accountable to God and there are standards of right and wrong. Paul says expect opposition and silence them by your lifestyle. Live in accordance with your teachings so that they will be ashamed because they cannot find something bad to say about you.

Older Men

"Teach the older men to be temperate, worthy of respect, self-controlled, and sound in faith, in love and in endurance" (Titus 2:2). By "older men" Paul isn't referring to someone who has one foot in the grave. He is talking to mature Christians who are older in the faith. If you have been a Christian for many years, you have influence on younger Christians.

Be Temperate

"Teach the older men to be temperate," Paul says. The King James version says "sober." The *Living Bible* says "serious." Temperate doesn't mean you can't laugh, but it means that you take life seriously. You realize that there is something more important than the next ball game, fishing trip, golf outing or horse race. Young men need to see Christians who can laugh and have fun but can also pray and talk about their faith, who live as if their relationship with God is the most important thing in their lives.

> Young men need to see Christians who live as if their relationship with God is the most important thing in their lives.

Be Worthy of Respect

In many Asian cultures older people are highly respected. Grandparents are cared for in the home and admired for their wise counsel. But in our culture, we idolize youth and vitality. Paul Harvey used to tell about the old man who put braces on his false teeth so he would look younger! Ads for hair color say, "This will return your hair to its natural color." Gray is not natural?

We tend to worship youth and show disrespect for aging people. If you're young, remember not to ridicule older people. Don't mock the way they walk or make fun of the way they drive. The Bible says you reap what you sow (Gal 6:7). Unless you die young, you will be there some day. If you're an older Christian, be worthy of that respect.

Be Self-Controlled

Make it easier for people to respect you by being self-controlled. The word for self-controlled is sometimes defined as "moderate in opinions or passions." Don't be overwhelmed by sudden wild alarms. Remain level-headed. Have a steadying influence on others. The *Living Bible* says, ". . . be unruffled."

Be Sound in the Faith

Some young Christians are vulnerable to every new spiritual fad. They want to be cutting edge, intellectually astute, and accepted by their peers. They need to be able to respect some older Christians in the church who are not tossed about by every wind of doctrine (Eph 4:14).

Practice Love

Some older Christians get crotchety and super dogmatic. But a wise Christian becomes more unselfish and more compassionate with age, continuing to have a positive influence on younger people.

Practice Endurance

We have a dangerous practice in America called *retirement*. After retiring from being the senior minister at Southeast Christian Church in 2006, I now know from firsthand experience that retirement is a blessing in many ways. But it is also dangerous because "retirement" implies that your productivity stops at a certain point.

Some church members look forward to retiring so that they can not only have freedom from daily work responsibilities but so they can get out of their volunteer roles as well. They think after retirement they are entitled to relax and travel and do everything for themselves for a while. You may want to refocus your interests and redirect your involvement in church, but don't quit! Don't turn over all the work and responsibility to the younger generation. The church needs the vitality of youth, but we also need the example and wisdom of the older people.

> "Retirement" implies that your productivity stops at a certain point.

The Bible has many examples of people who kept enduring until the end. Abraham's wife Sarah was 90 when she gave birth to Isaac. Moses was 80 when he led the children of Israel out of Egypt. Caleb was 85 when he conquered the hill country in Palestine. Simeon was an old man when he held the baby Jesus in the temple.

History has many examples as well. Picasso was past 75 when he dominated the art world. George Bernard Shaw was still writing plays when he was 90. Michelangelo did some of his best painting after 80. Norman Vincent Peale preached well into his 90s. Ronald Reagan was president in his late 70s.

A few years ago Bob Buford wrote a book entitled, *Halftime: Changing Your Game Plan from Success to Significance.*[1] In the book he suggested that many people in America today are successful enough that they can retire early and devote the second half of their lives to significant ministry without it costing the church a dime. At Southeast, for years our most significant volunteers have been older people. Key volunteers like Larry Taylor and Clark Esser devote forty hours a week or more to the church without taking a salary. They work harder than many of the paid staff! What a blessing and inspiration they are to the congregation.

> Older people can perform a great service to the Kingdom of God after retirement.

We've witnessed that older people can perform a great service to the Kingdom of God after retirement. They can clean the worship center, teach classes, babysit the next generation of leaders in the nursery, go on mission trips, fund mission trips for others, sit on committees, minister to the hurting, maintain the church grounds, and on and on.

If God permits you to live a long time, continue to serve him and be an inspiration to those who are younger. The Bible says, "He who stands firm till the end will be saved" (Matt 10:22).

Older Women

"Likewise, teach the older women to be reverent in the way they live, not to be slanderers or addicted to much wine, but to teach what is good" (Titus 2:3).

Years ago The Golden Girls was a television sitcom based on the premise that it's funny when older women are irreverent. Just the opposite is true. Once you get over the shock factor, there's not much humor in raunchy old women. But there is something very attractive about respectful, spiritual older women who are faithful in the Lord.

Don't Be Slanderers

Paul told Titus to teach the older women not to be slanderers. Gossip is a temptation for everyone, but it is a particular temptation for older women, perhaps because they have more time and opportunity to delve into others' lives. When we spread malicious tales, it sets a terrible tone for younger Christians. Be wise about hiding behind prayer requests or sharing "concerns" that are often cloaked forms of gossip. Be an example of talk that encourages people. "Do not let any unwholesome talk come out of your mouths, but only what is helpful for building others up according to their needs, that it may benefit those who listen" (Eph 4:29).

Don't Be Addicted to Alcohol

Paul also suggested older women should not be "addicted to much wine." Stuart Brisco once said, "The older women who turn to drink, as many of our soap operas document daily, are usually desperately lonely women who have no significant involvement in life. They feel unwanted and useless, grovel in feelings of inferiority and irrelevance, and show their inner disgust and loathing by carefully calculating self-destructive behavior."

I once knew a Christian woman whose husband died after she retired. She was despondent. Completely out of character, she began to drink during the day to boost her spirits. Soon she began to drink before going to bed so she could relax and fall asleep. Her friends saw her personality change, but they didn't know what was causing it. Eventually her alcoholism caused her to lose the positive reputation she had built in the church. She was not a good example to the younger women.

If alcohol is threatening to destroy your life, make a change. Say, "It's gone far enough. I'm going to contact Alcoholics Anonymous or my minister." Do it for your own sake, for the sake of your family, and most importantly for the Lord and your testimony. Alcoholism is the one disease that has to be self-diagnosed to be treated.

Teach What Is Good

When older women live a righteous life, they are in a position to "teach what is good" as Paul suggested. In the next chapter we'll dig deeper into what the older women should teach. Remember what is said of the ideal woman, "Charm is deceptive, and beauty is fleeting; but a woman who fears the LORD is to be praised. Give her the reward she has earned, and let her works bring her praise at the city gate" (Prov 31:30-31).

More than 40 years ago I read a book by J. Wallace Hamilton that really influenced me. One chapter was titled, "How Long Is Your Shadow?" The shadow to which he referred is our influence. He said we can't control the extent of our influence any more than we can stop having a shadow in the sun. He made two great points that have always stayed with me.

First, he said that your influence, for the most part, is unconscious. You're not conscious of your shadow when you walk down the street, but it is there. You hardly ever think of your influence on others, but it is still there. Typically we think our influence over people is determined by our performance or our intentional conversations, but in reality, we exert great influence when our guard is down.

> Your influence, for the most part, is unconscious. We exert great influence when our guard is down.

We say, "My kids are growing up so fast. I need to influence them." So we sit them down and lecture them about clean living and their belief in God. We say, "Now I've done it, I've influenced my kids." Maybe, because everyone needs those important conversations sometimes. But that's not really where the influence lies. What influences them the most is not our speech when we're trying to impress them, but our casual conversations when we're not even paying attention.

Second, Hamilton said your influence is almost immortal. Like the ripples that flow out from a pebble thrown into the pond, your influence goes far beyond your ability to see. You touch one life, then that life touches another, and then another. Even a person's death does not destroy his or her shadow of influence. J. Wallace Hamilton died in 1968, but his shadow continues to be cast because of the influence he had on me, and the influence I in turn had on others. A person may write a book, leave a will, or just leave a memory, but though his voice is silent, he goes on speaking through his lengthened shadow. Who knows how your life is going to influence someone way down the road?

In the late 1800s my great-grandmother was a divorcée with three small children in a day when divorce was a terrible stigma. But she refused to give up on her influence. Every Sunday morning she got her three children dressed and took them to church. One of those children was my grandfather who as an adult became a leader in his church. My grandfather laid his hands on me when I was ordained and prayed for me. How much do I, and any person who has been influenced by my ministry, owe to a woman in the late 1800s whom very few people even noticed? We won't know till heaven.

Hamilton suggested that's why we won't be judged immediately when we die. We have to wait till Judgment Day when all the returns are in. Even after our life here is finished, its influence will go on. Not until the end can you know how your shadow has impacted the total of the human race. 3:16

[1.] Bob Buford, *Halftime: Changing Your Game Plan from Success to Significance* (Grand Rapids: Zondervan, 1994).

Set the Example 4

Promoting Growth through Example

1. Who was your favorite teacher in school? Why? Is he or she still casting a shadow on your life? In what way?

2. This passage and the next speaks to "older men," "younger men," "older women," and "younger women." In which camp do you consider yourself? (Notice that in the context of the next passage, Titus 2:4, the younger women are those who still have children at home. That may help.)

3. If you are a younger man or woman, do you know any older men or women who exemplify the characteristics described in this passage? Do you show respect to them? How could you intentionally build a closer relationship with them?

4. If you are an older man or woman, are there younger people in your life whom God intends you to be mentoring? How could you earn the right to be heard? What are some ways you could invest more intentionally in their lives?

> **Memory Verse**
> **Titus 2:8**
>
> *In your teaching show integrity, seriousness and soundness of speech that cannot be condemned, so that those who oppose you may be ashamed because they have nothing bad to say about us.*

CHAPTER FIVE

PLAN FOR THE FUTURE

TITUS 2:4-8

Someone said, "If you want to make God laugh, tell Him your plans." People sometimes ask me what my vision was for Southeast Christian Church when we first began in 1966. Since there is so much talk today about setting goals and casting a vision, I think people expect me to say, "I envisioned all this from the beginning. I pictured 18,000 people attending every week, 2,000 additions a year, dozens of support groups, a 28-million-dollar annual budget, and 4.5 million dollars given to missions every year." But the truth is I didn't envision any of that. In fact, twenty years ago on a youth night one of our Bible college students said in a sermon that he foresaw 10,000 people worshiping at Southeast, and the congregation laughed. I laughed louder than anyone!

I don't want to underestimate the importance of setting goals, organizing future planning committees, and collecting data. Jesus said that no man builds a tower without first calculating the cost and no king goes to war without first estimating his odds of winning (Luke 14:28-32). But the Bible also says, "Many are the plans in a man's heart, but it is the LORD's purpose that prevails" (Prov 19:21). When I first came to Southeast, if you would have asked me about my vision for the church, I would have said, "I'd like to see this church become four or five hundred people and have a vital influence in this community." Sometimes if we told God our plans, he would laugh because he is preparing to do immeasurably more than we can imagine!

I'm not a great visionary, but I'm thankful for the leaders we had at the time who were. They didn't anticipate how much God would bless us, but they kept stretching, imagining, walking by faith, and taking risks. It was not our plans but good leadership, along with a lot of circumstances beyond our control, which created the fertile soil for God to bless us to the extent that he did.

Since no one can predict the future except God alone, the best way to plan for the future is for today's leaders to invest their time and energy encouraging and mentoring young people who can make wise decisions and who will follow God with integrity when the present leadership is no longer around.

Train Young Women

In the last chapter we discussed how Paul emphasized the importance of godly older women in the church. In the next sentence, Paul explains why this is so vital: "Then they can train the younger women to love their husbands and children, to be self-controlled and pure, to be busy at home, to be kind, and to be subject to their husbands, so that no one will malign the word of God" (Titus 2:4).

Women have the freedom in our culture to choose just about any career they want to choose. But many godly young women are recognizing an old truth: "The hand that rocks the cradle rules the world."

> "The hand that rocks the cradle rules the world." The home is where our best discipleship occurs.

In many churches today there is a renewed emphasis on the importance of family, and with good reason. The home is where our best discipleship occurs and where the future of our church resides. Older women can play a vital role by spending time with the younger women in the congregation, helping them with their busy schedules, and training them to be the women God has called them to be. Paul mentions several specific characteristics the older women should seek to develop in the younger women.

Love Your Husband and Children

In television advertisements, pop music, sitcoms, and movies, our culture tells young women, "Your husband is stupid and your children are in the way." Young women needed to be reminded by the teaching and example of older women that God calls us to love and respect one another.

In this passage Paul uses the Greek word *phileo*, not *agape*, to describe the kind of love young women should have for their husbands and children. *Agape* means showing unconditional love, doing the loving thing whether you like it or not. But *phileo* has to do with friendship. Teach younger women to delight in their family relationships, to enjoy their roles, and develop friendships with their spouses.

Be Self-Controlled and Pure

It is absolutely essential to the well-being of children, and consequently to the passing on of our faith to the next generation, that their mother have high moral standards. It has been said that children can sometimes survive a bad father, but they seldom survive a bad mother. When a mother is unfaithful to her husband or unfaithful to the Lord, she not only endangers her marriage, she endangers the well-being of her children as well. Children need their mother to consistently set the moral tone in the home.

> Children can sometimes survive a bad father, but seldom a bad mother.

My mother once did something when I was a young boy that embarrassed me at the time, but now I take pride in it. We had invited over some guests, and we were all crowded into the living room watching a program on our new television. Something suggestive came on the television. I don't remember exactly what it was—probably something that would be considered very mild by today's standards, like a two-second kiss. But I remember that everybody felt a little awkward. My mother got up, flipped off the television, and said, "Let's talk." It was amazing—everybody started jabbering at once as if they weren't really interested in the program anyway! I was a little embarrassed by my mother's actions at the time, but I'm proud now to look back and see her moral courage. The Bible says, "Finally, brothers, whatever is true, whatever is noble, whatever is right, whatever is pure, whatever is lovely, whatever is admirable—if anything is excellent or praiseworthy—think about such things" (Phil 4:8). I never questioned my mother's purity of thought or life. It's no wonder she had a tremendous impact on the young women around her.

Put Family First

Paul says the older women should teach the younger women "to be busy at home" (Titus 2:4). Researcher George Barna discovered that very few people change their minds about spiritual things when they grow up. In fact, he said, "a person's moral foundations are generally in place by the time they reach age *nine*"![1] If that is true, then intentionally spending quality time with our children when they are very young is vital to assuring that our faith is passed on.

That's why I've always advised mothers of young children to try not to have a job outside the home. I'm thankful that there is a trend among Christian women toward staying at home with their kids in the early years. Being busy at home doesn't exclude young women from doing things that benefit the family financially. Lydia was a seller of purple. Priscilla worked making tents. The virtuous woman in Proverbs 31 was involved in real estate and trading merchandise. But in order to develop the next generation of Christian leaders, a young woman's priority—the bulk of her time and energy—should be spent on being a wife and mother.

Unfortunately, many times a young mother feels like she doesn't have a choice but to work outside her home. Her husband says she must get a job in order to make ends meet. Or maybe her parents are demanding that she keep the career they worked so hard to help her achieve through college tuition. Young families have difficult decisions to make sometimes. Husbands and wives together should decide that for the sake of the Kingdom of God, their children will be a priority, even if that means going without certain things or disappointing her parents. And the rest of us should refrain from casting judgment no matter what a young woman's decision in this area might be.

The best way older women can train younger women to be busy at home is by helping out! Being a mother of small children can be draining and discouraging. When times were simpler, the older and younger women lived close together and the older women naturally pitched in to help. Times are different, but that means there is great opportunity for ministry and influence. When an older woman offers to babysit some small children one evening so a young couple can go on a date, or cook a meal for a nursing mother, or do a load of laundry, or help clean house, she endears herself to that young mother and earns the right to be heard. In those situations where a young woman must work outside the home, the need and the opportunity for ministry are even greater. Rather than cast judgment, lend a helping hand so that your influence on the next generation will increase.

Be Kind

Paul says the older women should teach the younger women how to be kind. Do you ever wonder why we treat strangers with kindness and tenderness, but snarl continually at the people we're going to weep over the most when they die? The Bible says, "Be kind to one another." A mother can often set the tone for this attitude in the home by her example. If your attitude is surly, sarcastic, and critical, then your home is not going to be a very pleasant place. But if you are gentle, encouraging and kind, then the home has a much better chance of being a place of peace.

As I mentioned earlier, the culture teaches young women to be sarcastic and mean-spirited toward their husbands. Older women can further encourage that destructive behavior, or they can teach the younger women by their example and creative advice how to be kind.

> Older women can encourage destructive behavior, or teach kindness by their example.

Be Submissive

Older women should also teach the younger women to "be subject to their husbands." It is a basic biblical principle that the husband is to be the leader in the home. The Bible does not command all women to be subject to all men, but a wife is to be submissive to her husband. That doesn't mean the husband should be a dictator like Ralph Kramden or Archie Bunker.[2] The Bible also commands husbands to love their wives as Christ loves the church (Eph 5:25). He is to be a leader and a tender-hearted lover. But there is to be an acknowledged order in the home even when he is imperfect.

On a football team, the quarterback is the one who calls the plays even though he may not be the smartest, strongest, or fastest player on the team, because the coach has designated him to be the play caller. The husband is in the role of leadership even when the wife is more capable in many areas. That takes a lot of humility on the part of the wife. But Jesus was obedient to his parents and respectful of the authorities in his life even though he was a much greater person than they. In the same way, a wife is supposed to imitate Christ and respect the authorities in her life.

Every wife has a choice to make. She can build her home as the world does, saying, "This is a partnership. I have full rights. Nobody tells me what to do." Or she can say, "We will try to build this home the way God designed. When we have disagreements, I want to feel free to express my point of view, but if we can't come to agreement, I'll acknowledge your leadership." That humble attitude eliminates the constant tug-of-war so prevalent in marriages today.

I once read a portion of a book by Gene Getz commenting on this subject. He suggested that often when a woman has difficulty submitting to her husband, she has difficulty submitting to other authorities as well—her boss, her elders, her governing officials. The underlying issue is not one of rights but of pride. She has an attitude of defiance toward all authority instead of humbly submitting to God's delegated authorities as we all are commanded to do. Certainly some authorities are more difficult to submit to than others, but think of the biblical characters who made a great impact because of their willingness to submit to the authorities in their lives even when it was difficult—Sarah, Joseph, David, Nehemiah, Esther, Daniel, Jesus, and many others.

A young mother needs a lot of encouragement in this area, because she is being barraged with messages from the culture telling her just the opposite of what the Bible tells her. She needs some older women mentoring her by their examples and encouraging her that being kind and submissive at home doesn't mean being a doormat but means having a humble spirit and respecting the authority she has been given.

For the Glory of God

A young mother's motivation for developing this kind of spirit in her home is "so that no one will malign the word of God." There is no greater testimony to our faith in Jesus Christ than a Christian home. Skeptics can try to ridicule the Bible; they can make fun of televangelists; but they will not ridicule a godly home. Over and over again even unbelievers will say, "I wish my home were like that."

A mother's motivation is not just to convince the skeptics, but more importantly her own children. Our primary purpose—perhaps the greatest way to impact the Kingdom of God on earth—is to raise children who know Jesus Christ. If children sense that their mother is hypocritical, they will grow up to malign the Word of God and ridicule the church. But if they know their mother's faith is genuine, even though she's imperfect, they will grow up to respect the Bible and love the church.

Young mothers need the reinforcement and encouragement that older women can provide. Especially in an era when so many young women did not grow up in a godly home, older women in the church can play a vital role in the lives of young mothers. Constantly remind them that they are performing the most important job in the church by raising their young children to know Jesus, and assist them in this great occupation so the next generation will know our Lord.

Train Young Men

After all these directives toward young women, Paul simply says, "Similarly, encourage the young men to be self-controlled" (Titus 2:6).

Help Them Grow Up

Certainly we need to teach young men other things, but Paul mentions only self-control. Maybe the people on the island of Crete were out of control. Or maybe Paul knew that there is one trait that young men need to learn, and that many of the others will fall into place if they will maintain self-control. Many men who would have made great leaders in the church have ruined their influence on their children and have limited their potential impact for the Kingdom because they lacked self-control in their younger years.

All kinds of outside influences seek to control our young men. Some are controlled by chemicals; they're so driven by their desire for drugs or alcohol that they do senseless things. Some are driven by their craving for sex and they lose all sense of judgment. Some are driven by greed or pleasure and lose all common sense. But we must train our young men that they are to be distinctive. They must learn that their primary mission in life is not to have fun but to be obedient. They must learn that the will of God and His church come before personal ambition.

> We must train our young men that their primary mission in life is to be obedient; and our young ladies not to marry men stuck in "perpetual adolescence."

We need to teach our young men that it is good and right for them to grow up. Dr. Albert Mohler and others have written about the "perpetual boyhood" of today's young men. Jewish and Christian cultures knew nothing of adolescence. When a boy physically became a man, he was expected to act like one. But a generation ago our society began to allow young men to experience a phase of "adolescence," during which they could still act like children. Suddenly a young man could do what he wanted until he was 18, or maybe even 21, and get by with it because he was not yet an adult. Now, a generation later, men can act like boys well into their 30s with little consequence. We should teach our young ladies not to marry men who are stuck in this "perpetual adolescence." And we should teach our young men that the church and the world need them to accept the responsibilities of adulthood, grow up, and be self-controlled.

Encourage Them

Paul says the young men need to be *encouraged* to be self-controlled. Stuart Briscoe says the word *encourage* in this passage means "persuade with authority." Don't have a casual attitude when you see a young man with great potential getting off track. Use your authority and persuade him to return to right living. Most of the time young people need what educators call "positive encouragement." Catch them being good. If you encourage them when their behavior is correct, they'll be more likely to repeat it. But sometimes young men need chastisement. They need someone who will love them enough to speak the truth. If you are usually positive, your occasional corrections will hold a lot more sway over a young man with great leadership potential.

When my son Rusty graduated from high school in the mid 1980s and was heading off to Bible College, Russ and Jane Summay of our church gave him a card that said they were going to send him 50 dollars a month for every month he was in Bible College. For four straight years, faithfully they sent a note each month with a check for 50 dollars. His dad didn't make much money at the time, so Rusty really appreciated that gift! Imagine the anticipation he felt every month waiting for that check to arrive and the encouragement he received from that gift. I was thankful too because without that money he wouldn't have come home nearly as often!

Rusty is in the ministry primarily because he feels called by God. But he says that in moments of doubt and frustration, he was motivated to stay faithful to the Lord and to his Bible college education because he didn't want to disappoint people like Russ Summay who had encouraged him and sacrificed for him. You can also bet that when Russ Summay had a word of correction for Rusty, it meant a lot more than if someone else had said it. Older people in the church can have a tremendous impact on future leaders if they will creatively encourage young people and occasionally offer corrective criticism.

Exemplify Good Leadership

> In everything set them an example by doing what is good. In your teaching show integrity, seriousness and soundness of speech that cannot be condemned, so that those who oppose you may be ashamed because they have nothing bad to say about us (Titus 2:7-8).

As we discussed in the last chapter, young people learn best by example. That means we must constantly be on guard, alert that people are watching our example and learning from it. Someone once asked superstar baseball player Joe DiMaggio why he hustled all the time. He said, "I know that every time I go out on the field somebody in the stands is seeing me play for the first time. I don't want to disappoint them."

Paul said, "In everything, set them an example by doing what is good." One of the things that should motivate Christians to give their best every day is the example they're setting. Somebody is always observing you. When you least expect it, they're watching you and imitating your ways.

I can hardly go anywhere without people recognizing me. It doesn't bother me when people say hello in public. What does bother me is realizing later how many people saw me but said nothing. Later they will say, "I saw you on the expressway behind that older lady who wouldn't merge. You were really irritated with her!" Or, "I watched you when the Ladybirds danced at halftime of the basketball game. You were a little too interested!" They don't believe me when I tell them I was looking for someone on the other side of the court! People are always watching, so we should give our best all the time in order to encourage young people to imitate our ways and be self-controlled.

A few years ago in the midst of several scandals involving religious leaders, *Christianity Today* reported that Billy Graham had remained America's most admired religious leader. When asked how he avoided the sexual and financial scandals that had plagued other ministries, Billy Graham replied,

> I decided that there were three areas where Satan could attack in—pride, morals and finances. Over the years, I tried to set up safeguards against the dangers of each. . . . From the earliest days, I've never had a meal alone with a woman other than Ruth, not even in a restaurant. I've never traveled in a car alone with a woman [other than my wife].[3]

The article went on to explain how Billy Graham has protected himself financially by taking a modest salary from his organization, not taking speaker's fees, and giving away all of his book royalties. He said that from the beginning of his ministry, "I was frightened—and still am—that I could do something that would dishonor the Lord."

Future leaders are examining your life very closely, even when you think nobody is looking. They don't expect you to be perfect, but they want to follow a person who is authentic and full of integrity. Your message means nothing if there is not a legitimate lifestyle behind it. Paul said, "In your teaching show integrity, seriousness and soundness of speech that cannot be condemned" (Titus 2:7,8). 3:16

---

[1] George Barna, "Research Shows That Spiritual Maturity Process Should Start at a Young Age" (November 17, 2003), http://www.barna.org/FlexPage.aspx?Page=BarnaUpdate&BarnaUpdateID=153. Emphasis mine.

[2] On the classic television program, *The Honeymooners*, Ralph (played by Jackie Gleason) used to threaten his wife Alice with a fist-propelled trip "to the moon," and on *All in the Family*, Archie (played by Carroll O'Connor) was constantly telling Edith to "stifle."

[3] Billy Graham, *Christianity Today*, 32:17 (Nov. 18, 1988) 21-23.

Promoting Growth by Planning for the Future

1. In your congregation, do the older people and younger people have much interaction with one another? If not, what could you do to facilitate some natural relationship-building between the different generations represented in your church?

2. Paul says the older women should "train" the younger women. How should this happen—formally, informally or both? How is it happening in your congregation?

3. Is motherhood honored in your congregation? Do the young women aspire to this great occupation? If not, how can your church, especially the older women, change this perception?

4. What characteristics in a young man indicate leadership potential? Do you know of anyone who possesses this potential? How can you encourage him?

5. Share some of your dreams about your church's future. What is different? What is the same? What kind of leaders do you have? Are there young people currently in your congregation you envision leading some day? What would your church have to do to accomplish those dreams? What should your part be?

Memory Verse
Titus 2:7

In everything set them an example by doing what is good.

CHAPTER SIX

MAKE CHRISTIANITY ATTRACTIVE IN THE MARKETPLACE

TITUS 2:9-10

Imagine your favorite football team is in a huddle. They're behind by four points with ten seconds to go, and they are one yard away from scoring a touchdown. Everyone knows the next play is crucial. But the team just stays in the huddle and talks. The referee finally blows the whistle, throws a flag and steps off a five-yard penalty for delay of game. But the team still stays in the huddle, holding hands and talking. Finally they burst out of the huddle cheering wildly as if they just did something significant. Then they run to the sidelines and out of the stadium, climb in their cars and go home! Every fan would be livid with that kind of behavior because a huddle is not an end in itself. The purpose of the huddle is to plan the strategy for the next play and to encourage those who are participating. A team would never just huddle and then hurry home.

But sometimes that's an accurate portrayal of the church. Once a week we gather for worship. Christians should worship—that's a special time when we honor our Coach, seek to discover his strategy for our lives, and encourage one another. But some of us see that gathering as an end in itself. We measure a church's effectiveness by the number of people in the holy huddle and by the level of inspiration in that hour. Then we disperse and disappear until the next week,

> **There is a spiritual battle going on in which Jesus expects us to engage.**

59

forgetting that there is a spiritual battle going on in the world in which Jesus expects us to engage.

Jesus said, "You are the salt of the earth. But if the salt loses its saltiness, how can it be made salty again? It is no longer good for anything, except to be thrown out and trampled by men" (Matt 5:13). The purpose of salt in Jesus' day was not only to add flavor but to preserve the meat as well. It has to penetrate the meat in order to do its job. The purpose of the church is to make a difference in the world, but we have to penetrate the world in order to accomplish that goal. The effectiveness of the church is not measured by what goes on in worship, but by what goes on in the lives of church members throughout the week.

Paul discusses this basic truth in Titus 2:9,10, where he writes, "Teach slaves to be subject to their masters in everything, to try to please them, not to talk back to them, and not to steal from them, but to show that they can be fully trusted, so that in every way they will make the teaching about God our Savior attractive."

Thankfully, I doubt that anyone reading this book is a slave. But many of us are employed by someone. The principles Paul sets forth for slaves are applicable to us all, especially as we think about our jobs. Paul told slaves to perform their jobs in such a way that they would be magnets, attracting people to Christ. If we can grasp Paul's point, it will make a big difference in how we view the church and our everyday responsibilities.

Christianity Is to Permeate Every Area of Life

Paul addresses how Christian slaves should perform when they're at work, saying they should be "subject to their masters" and do their job in a respectful and trustworthy way. Many people want to segment life into categories like a *Time* magazine. They want there to be a section called Sports, a segment on Business, a different category called Entertainment, and in the back they'll reserve a section for Religion. They want to isolate religion from everyday life.

For example, educators will say, "Moral values should be taught in the home or in the church, but we are in the business of education—teaching facts. We need to have a values-free sex education course because it's not our job to teach values." Politicians will say, "I am personally against abortion, but I don't want to impose my religious values on the American people. That's a private matter." Businessmen say, "Going to church is fine, but don't mix business and religion or you will lose your shirt every time."

People in the world don't mind if we meet in a huddle and talk, but they don't want our faith to permeate other areas of life. Unfortunately, many Christians would prefer it that way, too. They want to be able to go to church for an hour of inspiration on Sunday mornings and then do as they please the rest of the week.

But our Lord Jesus Christ intended for our faith to dominate every facet of our lives. The Bible says, "Whatever you do, whether in word or deed, do it all in the name of the Lord Jesus. . ." (Col 3:17). Christ is "the head of the body, the church . . . so that in everything he might have the supremacy" (Col 1:18). Christianity is to permeate every area of your life. Paul said slaves should be "subject to their masters in everything," so that "in every way" we will represent Christ properly. *Everything!* When you accept Jesus Christ as your personal Savior, you also accept him as Lord. He's not just Lord for one hour of praise on Sunday mornings, he is Lord of all. He wants to be Lord not only of your religious life, but also of your entertainment life, your school life, your date life, your work life.

We should tell potential members of our congregations, "Before you commit your life to Jesus and to his body the church, understand what is expected of you. You are not just expected to attend services regularly and give a little bit of your money and invite your neighbor if you think the program will be good. That's good, but it's only a small beginning. As a follower of Jesus and a representative of this church, you are expected to make Jesus Christ your Lord in every aspect of your life. We don't expect you to be perfect—none of us is perfect. But we do expect you to be guided by God's Word and to acknowledge the authority of Jesus Christ in every facet of your existence. We do not expect you to have it all together before coming to Jesus. You have to trust that he will transform you. But you have to come with a submissive spirit, with a desire to follow him as Lord."

Christianity is a new way of thinking, feeling, and behaving about everything. If it is true that God created us, then he's the Lord of everything. If it is true that Jesus Christ died to save us from our sins and from hell, then that message is needed by everyone. If it is true that Christ rose from the dead and promises a perfect, eternal life to those who abide in him, then that hope should dominate our lives every day.

> Christianity is a new way of thinking, feeling, and behaving about everything.

Suppose you are working as a cook in a restaurant when a fire breaks out in the kitchen. Out in the dining room, everybody is relaxed and having a good time. But if you care about people, you will interrupt them. "Ladies and gentlemen," you say, "may I have your attention, please?" Momentarily you will be conspicuous and people may resent you. The patrons don't want their meals interrupted, the waiters don't want to lose their tips, and the owner doesn't want the establishment to receive a negative image. But if you believe you have a message that will save lives, you will risk that momentary resentment.

If Christianity is true, it affects everything and everybody. That's why when the early Christians were told not to preach any more in the name of Jesus, they said, "We can't help but speak about what we've seen and heard." No area of life can be unaffected by Jesus Christ. The world may not like that idea, but it's the truth. In everything, Christ is to have supremacy. We are to be his representatives every minute in every place.

> No area of life can be unaffected by Jesus Christ.

Allan Dunbar, the Executive Director of the North American Christian Convention, used to be on television throughout Canada when he preached in Calgary. Once when he was flying to Phoenix, Arizona, his plane stopped in Las Vegas for about 50 minutes. He didn't just want to sit on the plane since he'd never been to Las Vegas before, so he got out and walked around.

The airport was filled with slot machines, those "one-armed bandits." Allan had two quarters in his pocket. He thought, *I'm hundreds of miles from home. There's hardly anybody around and nobody will recognize me here.* He slipped two quarters into the slot machine and pulled the arm. Quarters came pouring out from everywhere, clanging into the tray! He gathered them up and stuffed them into his pockets. On the plane he counted 28 dollars in quarters. He was delighted!

When he landed in Phoenix and exited the plane, a man and his wife approached him. "Pastor Dunbar!" they said. "We watch you on television in Canada every week. We respect the Word you preach. You are really a man of God. We're here on vacation in Phoenix and we're waiting to meet our son who was on this same plane."

Just then their son also exited the plane and they introduced him to Pastor Dunbar. "Oh yes, Reverend," he said. "So how much did you make back there in Las Vegas?"

Our faith is to permeate our private life as well as our public life. We should not be duplicitous, doing things when we think nobody is watching that would detract from our Christian witness. Our home life, our church life, our jobs, even our entertainment should be subject to the Lordship of Christ. That may seem like a heavy responsibility, and it is. But in everything he is to have supremacy.

Our Responsibility Is to Attract Others to Christ

Paul said slaves should "make the teaching about God our Savior attractive" (Titus 2:10). The world's stereotype of a Christian is somebody who never has a good time and tries to prevent others from having a good time. Sometimes our attitude and our countenance justify that conclusion. I know some Christians who seem to be happy in church, but when they go out into the world and associate with non-Christians, they are so insecure that they can't enjoy themselves at all. If they ever approach a non-Christian about faith, they are so defensive that they come across as angry and condemning.

Artists often portray Christ with a weak and sad appearance, with long, matted hair, looking more like a heroine addict than a powerful leader. I think we need to erase that image from our minds. Though the Bible says there was nothing in Christ's appearance that would attract us to him (Isa 53:2), he had a charisma and power that drew people by the thousands. Jesus was a carpenter, and in those days carpenters had to fell their own trees. They were built like lumberjacks with calloused hands and broad shoulders. Jesus attracted and related to outdoorsmen like Peter, Andrew, James, and John. People from every other walk of life were attracted to Jesus. The blind beggar Bartimaeus, the aristocrat Nicodemus, the sinful woman at the well, and the pious rich young ruler all wanted to associate with Jesus. Little children and older people wanted to be near him. Crowds of more than 5,000 people would flock to hear him preach. That's the Jesus we are called to represent to the world.

In his last words to his disciples, knowing he was about to die, Jesus talked about the joy that was in him and the love that he felt for his friends, and that he wanted them to love one another as he had loved them (John 15:11,12). There should be an attractiveness about us—a peace, a love, a joy, and a vitality—that makes others look at us and say, "I want to know the Lord they know. They have something I don't have."

> There should be an attractiveness about us that makes others say, "I want to know the Lord they know."

I've always admired the way legendary singer and entertainer Pat Boone has been able to make Christianity attractive in the marketplace. He has managed to maintain his principles while keeping a good sense of humor and an attractive personality.

I once attended a program following the Foster Brooks Pro-Celebrity Golf Tournament in Louisville and Pat Boone was on the platform. The emcee, Gordie Tapp, told one raunchy story after another throughout the evening. When it finally came time for Pat Boone to sing a couple of songs, Pat said, "I came to this tournament because Foster Brooks came to my tournament in Chattanooga, where the proceeds go to a Christian orphanage. Foster asked me if he could tell a particular joke that night. I said, 'Well, Foster, that's funny, but that's probably not appropriate for this Christian audience.'

"Then Foster asked me about a second joke, and I said, 'Foster, that's funny too, but you had better not tell that one either.' By the time Foster got done screening his jokes, he only had about three minutes of material left."

Then Pat Boone turned to Gordie Tapp, the emcee. He said, "Gordie, if you had been there, you would have had to do a mime act!" I thought it was the funniest line of the night, and the audience appreciated it too. Pat had made his point while keeping his sense of humor. Jesus said, "Let your light shine before men, that they may see your good deeds and praise your Father in heaven" (Matt 5:16).

Our Job Presents a Significant Opportunity for Witness

Paul told slaves that their performance on the job had a direct correlation with attracting people to the Savior. The primary purpose of your job is not just to earn a living, but to be a witness to Jesus Christ. In your job you will often be surrounded by non-Christians who need the hope of Jesus, and by weak Christians who need reinforcement. Your primary responsibility on the job has nothing to do with the stated job description. Your first goal is to "make the teaching about God our Savior attractive."

Years ago Robert Mattox wrote a book, *The Christian Employee*, in which he suggested that God purposely arranges our lives so that we have to work with non-Christians.[1] We spend about 36 percent of our waking hours at work, which means we are spending a significant amount of our lifetime interacting with non-Christians. Yet sometimes, instead of recognizing that God has arranged our lives so that we can influence them, we complain about the worldly people we have to work with.

Christian BusinessMen's Committee is a popular ministry that encourages men to get involved in prayer and discipleship in the workforce. CBMC began many years ago as a response to a survey in the Chicago area that revealed businessmen were more likely to discuss spiritual things with a fellow businessman than with a family member or clergyman.[2] It's not the paid representatives that people believe; it's satisfied customers. Your job is an opportunity for you to be a missionary. A lot of Christians think that if they were really spiritual they would quit their secular jobs and become full-time missionaries. God does call some people into full-time church work, but he proba-

> It's not the paid representatives that people believe; it's satisfied customers.

bly has you right where he wants you on the mission field of the marketplace.

Paul gives several specific directions so that slaves—and Christian employees—can continue to be a positive influence for Christ.

Have a Submissive Spirit

"Teach slaves to be subject to their masters in everything," Paul said. That doesn't come naturally. From infancy we exhibit a rebellious spirit. Nobody likes to be told what to do. One business attempted to establish a drug testing program for some of their employees who were in certain sensitive positions. The employees immediately filed a grievance with the National Labor Relations Board. They said, "We don't take illegal drugs, but we don't want the company infringing on our rights to privacy and forcing us to take this test." Something in our spirit rebels against authority.

Christian employees should instead exhibit a compliant spirit at work. Learn to repress your pride and respect delegated authority. Peter told Christian slaves to be obedient to their masters even when they were harsh or unreasonable (2 Pet 2:18). How much more should we, when we voluntarily take a position, have a submissive spirit toward those in authority over us?

One of the teenage boys in our church once brought a couple of his teachers and a school administrator to church with him. They had been so impressed by his polite spirit and submissive attitude at school that they respected his invitation to come to church. If he had been defiant in school, they would never have come.

Try to Please Your Boss

Paul says slaves should "try to please" their masters. Sometimes we're afraid that if we try to please those who are superior to us, we'll be accused of being a brown-noser. We bend over backwards not to do that because we want to be liked by our peers; ultimately we're trying to please ourselves rather than be obedient to God.

Think about Joseph who always sought to please those in authority. He obeyed his father even though his brothers hated him for it. Have you ever wondered if the other slaves in Potiphar's house resented him for pleasing Potiphar and rising to the top of the ranks? Did his fellow prisoners hate him for pleasing the jailer and being put in charge? Regardless of what his peers thought, Joseph determined to do the right thing. Our goal is not to please our peers but to obey God and to please His delegated authority in our lives.

Notice that Paul says we should "try" to please the boss. Some superiors can never be pleased, but as much as possible, try to be cooperative. Make your employer look good. Smile, have an upbeat spirit, and do your best all the time. That attitude will be so radically different from what they're used to seeing that they will be "attracted" to our Lord. In another passage, Paul wrote,

| **Make your employer look good.** |

> Slaves, obey your earthly masters in everything; and do it, not only when their eye is on you and to win their favor, but with sincerity of heart and reverence for the Lord. Whatever you do, work at it with all your heart, as working for the Lord, not for men, since you know that you will receive an inheritance from the Lord as a reward. It is the Lord Christ you are serving (Col 3:22-24).

You are not just serving a superior, you are serving the ultimate superior, Jesus Christ. When you rebel, you are rebelling against Jesus Christ. When you seek to please your boss, you are pleasing your Savior.

Guard Your Tongue

Paul says slaves shouldn't "talk back" to their masters. People talk back to their bosses in all kinds of subtle ways. They'll say, "That's not in my job description," or "I thought I did exactly what you told me to do," or "We've never done it that way here before." Or they will gripe and moan about how hard they have to work, making everybody around them—especially the boss—miserable. Or maybe instead of talking back to the boss's face, they complain behind his or her back.

"No man can tame the tongue," James said. "It is a restless evil, full of deadly poison" (Jas 3:8). Learn to control your tongue at work. Don't get involved in all the griping and rumors that are circulating. Anybody can gripe about how tough his job is, and somebody always will. Don't join in. You will give a good witness for Jesus Christ if you restrain your tongue.

Don't Steal Time or Money

Paul says to instruct slaves "not to steal" from their masters. A recent study revealed that over 79 percent of employees admitted they would steal from their employers if they could get by with it. "The loot is far more sophisticated than mere pens and paper clips," CNN said in its report on the study. "Computer software, office appliances and accounting books are all prime targets for would-be pilferers and grafters." One third of companies that go bankrupt each year do so as a result of employee theft, the article said, costing businesses between $60 billion and $120 billion a year. Interestingly, only 8 percent of employee thieves did it because of "need." Forty-nine percent said they did it out of greed, and 42 percent out of vindictiveness—a desire to get back at their employers.

And it's not just poor slaves who are tempted to steal. "For the most part, thieves run the demographic gamut," the article reported. One of the researchers said, "It goes all the way to the top. I've seen it from corporate vice presidents to janitorial staff." In fact the higher up the ladder an employee was, the more likely he was to steal a greater amount of money. "The whiter the collar, the bigger the dollar."[3]

If you refuse to steal from your employer, you will be in the extreme minority. Your employer will be grateful and Jesus Christ will get the glory.

> If you refuse to steal from your employer, you will be in the extreme minority.

Remember that as an employee, you can steal money by stealing time. I once heard about three boys who were arguing about whose dad was the fastest. "My dad can run a mile in less than six minutes," one boy said. "My dad can run a 40-yard dash in less than 5 seconds," the other said. "That's nothing," the third boy said. "My dad gets off work at 4:00 and is home by 3:30!

If you get paid to work 40 hours and you only work 35, you're stealing money you didn't earn. If you purposely loaf on the job and get by with as little work as possible, you're doing the same thing. Put in an honest day's work and don't steal time or money from your employer, so that people around you will be attracted to your Savior.

Be Fully Trustworthy

Slaves should "show that they can be fully trusted," Paul said. Demonstrate to your boss that you can be fully trusted. When Joseph was Potiphar's slave, the Bible says that Potiphar "left in Joseph's care everything he had; with Joseph in charge, he did not concern himself with anything except the food he ate" (Gen 39:6). Joseph was that dependable and trustworthy, and surely Potiphar was impressed with Joseph's God.

A slave owner once stood examining a young man who was on the auction block. He looked the slave in the eye and said, "If I buy you, will you be honest?"

The slave responded, "Sir, I'll be honest whether you buy me or not."

You may feel like a slave at times. But remember, slaves can have tremendous influence on those for whom and with whom they work. But we don't influence people nearly as much by carrying a big black Bible to work, having noontime Bible studies, and twisting people's arms, as we do by having a submissive and pleasant spirit, restraining our tongues, and being honest and trustworthy. When people see Jesus in you, they're attracted to him. So "whatever you do, whether in word or deed, do it all in the name of the Lord Jesus" (Col 3:17). 🔲

[1] Robert Mattox, *The Christian Employee* (Plainfield, NJ: Logos International, 1978).

[2] Eldon Kibbey, "CBMC—Connecting Business Men to Christ," *Indy Christian.com*, March 31, 2005. http://indychristian.com/2005_03_01_indychristian_archive.html.

[3] Nicole Jacoby, "Battling Workplace Theft," *CNN Money*, August 19, 1999. http://money.cnn.com/1999/08/19/investing/q_employeetheft/.

‡

C
H
A
P
T
E
R

6   *Make Christianity Attractive in the Marketplace*

Promoting Growth by Permeating the World

1. Have you been guilty of sectioning your life into different categories? Is there an area of your life you don't want to give over to the lordship of Christ? Are you willing to repent and change?

2. How do non-Christians see you? Are you mean-spirited and dogmatic, or do you make Christ attractive?

3. How do we balance truth and grace in relating to non-Christians? How can we make sure to speak out against injustices and unethical behavior but at the same time be winsome and attractive? Do you know anyone who does this well?

4. Of the five directives Paul gives to slaves, which is most difficult for you to put into practice at work? How could you do better?

5. What kind of relationship do you have with your boss? Was there anything in this chapter that convicted you? How could you repent or improve?

6. Think of someone at work you'd like to influence for Jesus. Take time to pray for him or her.

> **Memory Verse**
> Titus 2:9,10
>
> *Teach slaves to be subject to their masters in everything, to try to please them, not to talk back to them, and not to steal from them, but to show that they can be fully trusted, so that in every way they will make the teaching about God our Savior attractive.*

CHAPTER SEVEN

LIVE HOLY LIVES IN AN UNHOLY WORLD

TITUS 2:11-14

Moses had a tough job. His task was to lead the Hebrew slaves out of Egypt into the land of Canaan. It wasn't so difficult physically—they could walk the 350 miles in about three weeks, and God's miraculous power was there to help them overcome any obstacles. But the real challenge wasn't the physical move from Egypt to Canaan—it was the spiritual transition that had to take place in the hearts of the people. The Hebrew people had been slaves for 400 years. Their intellectual training was minimal, so they were not accustomed to thinking through their problems. Their moral values were poor; for four centuries, they had been exposed to the pagan lifestyle of Egypt, so they didn't have a good grasp on right and wrong. Their maturity was weak; they had lived from hand to mouth for so long that they were not accustomed to planning for the future and making sound judgments. It's difficult to lead people like that. They were shallow, rebellious, stubborn, impatient, and complaining. Moses was probably anxious to get it over with.

When they arrived at the Promised Land a few months later, they weren't ready to occupy that new territory. They didn't have faith in God. They were not responsible enough to develop a government, build a military, or manage a business. Maturity takes a while to develop. People need time to cope with freedom. It took the children of Israel forty years of wandering in the wilderness before they were ready for the Promised Land. But God wanted them to be a special people, distinctive from the nations around them, so he was willing to wait forty years till they were ready. He planned to use those Hebrew people to be the ones through whom the Messiah would come into the world. They needed to be conditioned to think, feel, and behave the way God wanted.

God is calling a special people out of the world today—the Church. Jesus Christ is our leader. His death on the cross has secured our freedom from the slavery of sin. We've walked through the waters of baptism. We've eaten the manna of the Lord's Supper. We drink of the rock of the Holy Spirit. We have God's Word, the Bible, to guide us every day. We're marching towards Heaven, where we will spend eternity with God. But even though we've been saved from the slavery of sin and are looking forward to the Promised Land of heaven, a difficult transition is occurring in our lives. We are to become like God in his holiness. Though salvation occurs immediately when we accept Jesus as Lord, *sanctification* is a process of purification that takes place over the rest of our lives on this earth.

> **God is calling a special people out of the world today—the Church.**

In this passage from Titus 2, Paul mentions that Christ "gave himself for us to redeem us from all wickedness and to purify for himself a people that are his very own. . ." (Titus 2:14). But it's difficult to be purified when we aren't separate from the world. We are to be in the world but not of it. One of the greatest needs of our churches today is for believers to understand their role—to live holy lives in a world that has gone wrong. In Titus 2:11-14 we receive instructions, incentives, and the ingredients necessary for us to live as the people of God in the midst of a pagan society. Paul writes,

> For the grace of God that brings salvation has appeared to all men. It teaches us to say "No" to ungodliness and worldly passions, and to live self-controlled, upright and godly lives in this present age, while we wait for the blessed hope—the glorious appearing of our great God and Savior, Jesus Christ, who gave himself for us to redeem us from all wickedness and to purify for himself a people that are his very own, eager to do what is good.

Difficult Instructions

The instructions are not easy to follow. Paul says we are to "say 'no' to ungodliness and worldly passions" and "live self-controlled, upright and godly lives" (Titus 2:12).

Live Holy Lives in an Unholy World 7

Say No to Worldly Passions

The Bible speaks of three common categories of worldly passions: "the lust of the flesh, the lust of the eyes, and the pride of life" (1 John 2:16, KJV). We could label them physical pleasure, material possessions, and human pride. Those three passions beat within the heart of every human being, and if uncontrolled, will eventually enslave us in demanding habits. It's especially difficult to say no to those things when everything about this present age is designed to stimulate worldly desires.

We are to say no to inappropriate physical pleasure. This present age is adept at stimulating physical desires, especially sexual temptations. Billboards catch your eye with provocative pictures. The television camera in an advertisement for a diet drink scans a near-naked body. Pornography is readily available on the Internet. It is difficult to say "no" day after day to such skillful attempts to arouse the flesh. A foreign churchman visiting America quipped, "Every day in America it is sex o'clock."

We are to say no to material possessions. This present age is also experienced at inflaming a passion for material possessions. Everywhere you go you are tempted to believe you need more things. The lottery says just a little more money will make you happy. Homearama says you can have this home and make all your dreams come true. Advertisements say you can take this dream vacation and really be fulfilled. Patrick Henry's cry was, "Give me liberty or give me death," but a few generations later we weakened it to just "Give me liberty," and now our cry is simply, "Give me."

> This present age is experienced at inflaming a passion for material possessions.

We are to say no to human pride. This present age is also an expert at inflaming status-consciousness. We have to wear the right clothes, shop at the right places, and drive the right cars. We spend money we don't have to buy things we don't need, to impress people we don't even like! Garry Trudeau, author of the Doonesbury cartoon strip, said in a commencement address at Colgate University, "We live in a world where we would rather be envied than esteemed. When we reach that place, may God help us."

We're to be the people of God. We are to say no to worldly passions no matter how attractive they may be at the moment, and that's not easy. But that's what Jesus did. Satan came to Jesus in the wilderness and said, "You're hungry, Jesus. Why don't you turn these stones into bread and eat it? You can satisfy your physical appetite."

Jesus said, "No, it is written, 'Man doesn't live by bread alone.'" Jesus knew there was something more important than what feels good.

Then Satan took him to a high hill and showed him all the kingdoms of the world in an instant and said, "If you will just bow down and worship me, I'll give you all these things."

Jesus said, "No, it is written, 'Worship God only.'" Jesus knew not to be attracted to the things of this world.

Then Satan took him to the pinnacle of the temple and said, "If you will just jump off, it is written in the Bible that the angels will catch you." What a spectacular stunt that would be, Satan was saying. People would come out to see that, Jesus! You could be famous!

But Jesus said, "No, it is written, 'Do not put the Lord your God to the test.'" Jesus said no to the temptation of pride.

Jesus proved that it is possible to say no to physical pleasure, material possessions, and worldly power. We can't do it on our own power, but with the Holy Spirit indwelling us, we have Christ's power. "For God did not give us a spirit of timidity, but a spirit of power, of love and of self-discipline" (2 Tim 1:7).

Say Yes to Godliness

Living holy lives in this world can be a difficult assignment not only because we are supposed to say no to temptation, but also because we're supposed to say yes to godliness. We are to "live self-controlled, upright and godly lives in this present age" (Titus 2:12).

If you are trying to improve your physical health, it is one thing to say no to chocolate sundaes. It is something else to say yes to broccoli and carrots and regular exercise. Jesus told a story about a man who cleaned an evil spirit out of his house only to leave it vacant, and seven evil spirits worse than the first came in to occupy it (Matt 12:43-45). We can't just say no to the passions of the world and leave ourselves in a vacuum. We have to say yes to positive living.

> We can't just say no to the passions of the world; we have to say yes to positive living.

Paul says to be "eager to do what is good" (Titus 2:14). The *Living Bible* paraphrases this verse, "We are to have a real enthusiasm for doing kind things for others." Jesus said no to the pleasures of this world, but then he went about doing good—healing the sick, ministering to the needy, teaching the truth. In fact the Bible says that "for the joy set before him" he endured the cross (Heb 12:2). He was eager to forgive sin. Like Jesus, we should be enthusiastic about loving people and doing good.

Powerful Incentives

Three powerful incentives for living godly lives are insinuated in this passage.

Remember God's Grace

"The grace of God that brings salvation has appeared to all men," Paul said (Titus 2:11). Jesus came into this world for the express purpose to die on the cross for our sins. He "gave himself for us to redeem us from all wickedness" (Titus 2:14). He died to buy us back, to redeem us. We are under God's grace and free from sin. But if we are saved from all of our sins, why not just go out and live like we want? Paul answered that question in Romans 6 when he wrote,

> What shall we say, then? Shall we go on sinning so that grace may increase? By no means! We died to sin; how can we live in it any longer? Or don't you know that all of us who were baptized into Christ Jesus were baptized into his death? We were therefore buried with him through baptism into death in order that, just as Christ was raised from the dead through the glory of the Father, we too may live a new life (Rom 6:1-4).

Suppose you had a son who developed a terrible gambling habit as a young man and stole thousands of dollars from you to pay for his debts. Suppose that he came and admitted his sin, asked for your forgiveness and offered to pay it back. Out of love for your son, knowing that he couldn't possibly afford to repay the debt, you tell him you forgive him and he doesn't have to pay it back. Your grateful child hugs you and thanks you profusely.

But then the next day you catch him gambling on the Internet. You ask him what he is doing and he nonchalantly says, "Oh, it's no big deal Pops, you've got me covered!" How would you feel? He has completely despised your grace and cheapened the sacrifice you made. He has not been truly repentant at all.

> **When we remember and appreciate God's grace, we are motivated to holy living.**

On the contrary, if he begins to work hard at his job, manage his money well, treat you kindly, and attend Gamblers Anonymous meetings, you are glad you forgave him. If he loves you, he is motivated to live rightly out of respect for the sacrifice you made.

When we remember and appreciate God's grace, we are motivated to holy living.

Understand God's Purpose

God's purpose is "to purify for himself a people that are his very own" (Titus 2:14). In the Old Testament, the Jews were to live distinctively among the heathen nations so that people could say, "Jehovah is the real God." Now God calls the Church to go out into the world and live distinctively pure lives so that others will say, "Jesus Christ is still alive."

I once saw a man on the beach who must have weighed over 300 pounds. His t-shirt read, "I conquered anorexia." What a living testimony! Nobody could deny the truth of his claim. People ought to see such distinctiveness in us that they can't deny the Lord has been working on us. When they see a loving marriage, disciplined children, honesty on the job, a joyful spirit, and kindness to others, they can say, "It is true—Jesus Christ is alive in those people."

The knowledge that you are a member of the Body of Christ, representing God in the world, should be an incentive for living rightly.

Believe God's Promise

A third incentive to living holy lives is our belief that Jesus is returning at any moment. Paul says we should live rightly "while we wait for the blessed hope—the glorious appearing of our great God and Savior, Jesus Christ. . ." (Titus 2:13). If the President of the United States were scheduled to visit your house, how would you prepare? You would clean the house and mow the lawn. You might even give the walls a fresh coat of paint and pay for some professional landscaping. When you understand that one day the Lord Jesus Christ, the King of kings, is coming to your house, you begin to beautify your life.

The first time Jesus came, people barely noticed; the next time he will come more dramatically—every eye will see. The first time he came in meekness; the next time he will come in authority—every knee will bow. The first time he came in love; the next time he will come in power and all his enemies will be put under his feet. In Joel 2:31, the Bible talks about the end of the world, speaking of "the great and dreadful day of the Lord." But in Acts 2, when Peter preaches the first gospel sermon, he quotes from Joel but calls it "the great and glorious day of the Lord." Whether that coming day is dreadful or glorious will depend on your relationship to Jesus Christ. You'll either be under his wrath or under his grace. If we're not under his grace, it will be a dreadful day. We need to purify our lives because the Lord will return one day.

> The first time Jesus came in love; the next time he will come in power.

‡

C
H
A
P
T
E
R

7

Live Holy Lives in an Unholy World

Years ago I preached a series of four sermons on the second coming. On the first Sunday of the series, I looked out and saw a man in the audience who I knew came from a worldly background. He hadn't been in church in years. I thought, *I'm not sure anything in this sermon will say to him what needs to be said or really touch his life.* But he came back the next Sunday and the next. Each week as I talked about the timing, the purpose, and the signs of the Lord's coming, I wondered if anything related to his life at all. Later he became a Christian. To my surprise he told me about the impact that series had on his life. He said, "That series of sermons on the second coming really put the fear of God in me!"

It's a strong motivator to realize that one day Christ is going to come in power, judgment, and glory—and we will face him and give account. "Since everything will be destroyed in this way, what kind of people ought you to be? You ought to live holy and godly lives as you look forward to the day of God and speed its coming" (2 Pet 3:11,12).

Essential Ingredients

Use Your Mind

Paul insinuates that there are a couple of essential ingredients to holy living. First, we are going to have to think. "The grace of God . . . teaches us" (Titus 2:11,12). We are told repeatedly in the Bible that Christians are to use their minds. Christ is the teacher; we are the disciples—we are learners. We are to be transformed by the renewing of our minds. We are to have the mind of Christ. Right thinking leads to right behavior and then to right feeling.

> Right thinking leads to right behavior and then to right feeling.

Our world is not accustomed to using the mind. The world primarily responds by instinct, passion, and emotion. Many let others do their thinking for them, and they parrot whatever their educators or people in the media taught them. As a result, there is a lot of confusion and chaos.

Billy Graham has a sermon called, "Facts, Faith and Feeling." The three need to go in that order. The facts should be understood, then we respond by faith, and then comes feeling.

When we make feeling our ultimate goal, we will be shallow people. That shallowness can have a very dangerous effect on the world around us and ruin our testimony. Charles Colson says that many German Christians broke down prior to World War II under the Nazi attack and renounced their faith or refused to stand up against injustices. The

Live Holy Lives in an Unholy World

exceptions were those like Bonhoeffer and Niebuhr who had thought deeply about their faith and knew where they stood. When faith is based on feeling, it falls apart when the pressure mounts because the

> When we make feeling our ultimate goal, we will be shallow people.

foundation is shaky. When it is based on the truth of God's Word and the historical reality of Christ, our faith can withstand great assaults and we can continue living holy lives despite the chaos around us.

Wait Patiently

This second ingredient may be tougher than the first. Paul said we live holy lives "while we wait for the blessed hope. . ." (Titus 2:13). Someone said maturity is "the ability to postpone pleasure." Most of the time the pleasures that tempt us aren't wrong in and of themselves, they're just wrong at the time. Sexual pleasure is a gift of God to be enjoyed in marriage, but it takes a godly, mature person to wait on God's timing. Material things are a blessing from God, but they are not to be acquired at the expense of the more important pursuit of godliness. God promised to exalt the humble, so it's not wrong to be exalted for God's glory, but it is wrong for that to be your pursuit and to lose patience while waiting on God's timing.

Our world is impatient. We want everything right now. We have instant coffee, instant meals, instant banking, and instant cameras. We communicate by computer and phone at the speed of light, and then we spend thousands of dollars so we can communicate even faster. I heard about a sign in Pennsylvania that read, "Antiques Made While You Wait." That's almost as dumb as the sign that read, "Ears Pierced While You Wait." Did they think I might take off my ears and leave them for a while?

Things that are worthwhile seldom come instantly. Maturity, character, wisdom, and holiness don't come quickly. Throughout the Scriptures God tells us, be patient for the coming of the Lord; wait on the Lord; they that wait on the Lord shall renew their strength; don't grow weary in doing good for in due season you will reap a harvest if you don't give up. Yet I find a lot of Christian people who are impatient. They pray, "Oh, Lord, my family is falling apart. I'm broke, I'm sick, my life is in shambles. Where are you? I'm trying to do what is right. I need you now!"

God urges us over and over again to be patient, to wait. Ultimately, He will win the victory. If not in this life, in the life to come, at "the glorious appearing of our Great God and Savior, Jesus Christ," he will make all things right.

Live Holy Lives in an Unholy World   7

For years those of us who knew Glen Wheeler have told a story about him similar to one that now often circulates on the Internet. Glen Wheeler was a preacher for a long time in Ironton, Ohio. When his wife passed away, Glen was almost lost for a while. He had grown to depend on her so much and he missed her badly.

"I miss the little things about her," he said. "After church when I was finished preaching and when everybody had gone, I would walk to the car with my wife. She would slip her arm in mine, and she would always say, 'You're a good man, Glen.' I miss hearing that.

"You know what else I miss?" he asked. "I miss her cooking." She was a great cook, and Glen's physique was a testimony to her success. "The great thing about meals was that so many times after we were finished, she would come around and pick up the plates, and she would say, 'Keep your fork, Glen.' I loved to hear her say, 'Keep your fork,' because that meant something better was coming. She made great desserts. I miss that."

Then Glen concluded, "Sometimes it's like I can hear the voice of God saying, 'Keep your fork, Glen. Just wait. The best is yet to come.'"

A Jewish refugee wrote an inscription on the wall of a cellar outside Cologne, Germany, during World War II, that read, "I believe in the sun, even when it is not shining. I believe in love even when feeling it not. I believe in God even when God is silent." Be patient. "They that wait upon the Lord shall renew their strength" (Isa 40:31, KJV). That can be a difficult thing in a world that has gone so wrong. But we are promised that if we wait, we will mount up with the wings of an eagle and fly someday. 3:16

Promoting Growth by Living Holy Lives

1. Which is easier for you to do—to say no to ungodliness or yes to godliness? Which is more important?

2. This chapter brought out three incentives to godly living. Which of those three is the most powerful motivator for you? Is there another powerful motivator that inspires you to holy living?

3. How do you define holy living? Name a person you think is living a holy life. What characteristics about him or her would you like to imitate?

4. Only the Holy Spirit can change and mold us into Christ's image. Yet there are some things we can do to make it harder or easier for the Spirit to do his work. When you consider the person you mentioned in question number 4, what disciplines have allowed him or her to be open to God's transforming power? Would you be willing to change your life so that these disciplines were a part of your life as well?

| **Memory Verse**
Titus 2:11,12 | *For the grace of God that brings salvation has appeared to all men. It teaches us to say "No" to ungodliness and worldly passions, and to live self-controlled, upright and godly lives in this present age.* |

Live Holy Lives in an Unholy World

CHAPTER EIGHT

RESPECT YOUR MINISTERS

TITUS 2:15

A minister's wife in a large congregation asked a new member if he was enjoying the church. He said, "Oh yes, it's great! I love the building, the music is terrific, and the people here have been warm and friendly."

"What about the preaching?" she asked.

"Well," he said, "that's one area I'm disappointed in. I think the preacher is a little dry. He preaches too long, and he really doesn't relate well to my life."

The minister's wife said, "Do you know who I am?"

He said, "No, I don't."

"I'm the minister's wife!" she said.

The stunned young man said, "Do you know who I am?"

She said, "No I don't."

"Good!" he said, and he disappeared into the crowd.

The ministry used to be a much more respected position than it is today. The minister was called the Parson, meaning "the person." The term historically meant a person of character, a person deserving respect. He was likely the most well-educated and well-traveled person in the community. But today the ministry has fallen into disrepute. Partly because of the moral failures of some prominent ministers, and partly because our society doesn't respect very many in authority, the American people don't hold the ministry in very high esteem any more. Paul told Titus, "These, then, are the things you should teach. Encourage and rebuke with all authority. Do not let anyone despise you" (Titus 2:15).

Paul told Titus to act with authority and not let anyone despise the office he held. If the church is to continue growing and changing lives, there must be a respect for the person at the helm.

The Minister's Identity

The paid preacher and staff of a congregation are called by different names. Sometimes he's called an evangelist. Most Bible scholars consider Titus an evangelist because that was the title given to Timothy who had a similar role (2 Tim 4:5). Paul said in Ephesians that God called some to be pastors and some to be evangelists (Eph 4:11), so they aren't exactly the same thing. An evangelist in Bible times seems to have been someone who was a church planter, whose role was short-lived, who was in charge of starting the church and appointing elders to govern it after he left.

In other congregations the minister is referred to as "Pastor." The term *pastor*, as we discussed in chapter two, is synonymous with *elder*. Sometimes in Scripture the minister is referred to as a paid elder or paid pastor. Paul told Timothy,

> The elders who direct the affairs of the church well are worthy of double honor, especially those whose work is preaching and teaching. For the Scripture says, "Do not muzzle the ox while it is treading out the grain," and "The worker deserves his wages" (1 Tim 5:17,18).

So we know it is permissible for a church to have a paid pastor whose primary responsibilities are preaching and teaching. In the New Testament churches, such a minister was not the only pastor, but one of a plurality of elders who oversaw the congregation.

That was my role at Southeast Christian Church for the forty years I served there. From the beginning the elders made it clear that my primary responsibilities were preaching and teaching, and they looked to me not as a hired hand nor as the dictator but as one among equals. That relationship served us very well and I can see the wisdom of God's Word in this area.

Sometimes the staff is simply called "ministers." I like that term because it means simply "servant." The terms *deacon, minister,* and *servant* come from the same Greek word in the New Testament, but the word did not always refer to the office of deacon. Timothy, who was an evangelist, was told to discharge the duties of his ministry. So the term could be used to refer to the work of church officials in various capacities much as we use the title

> Whether your paid leaders are called evangelists, pastors, or ministers, they deserve your respect.

Respect Your Ministers

"minister" today. Whether your paid leaders are called evangelists, pastors, or ministers, they are deserving of your respect as the ones God has ordained to lead the congregation.

William Enright compared the minister to a director of a symphony. His task is to blend the talents of the various members and produce a harmonious tune to the glory of God. But if the congregation thinks it is the minister's task to play every instrument, he is in trouble. There is no way he can study and preach and coach the ball team and run the website and visit the sick and call on new members and counsel married couples and perform weddings and funerals and be a youth sponsor and administer the budget and fill the baptistery and turn off all the lights and lock all the doors. In a smaller congregation he may attempt to perform all those functions. But he can't possibly do them all well, so he becomes vulnerable to criticism. His primary calling is being neglected and nobody is happy, including the minister.

The church needs to understand that we are all the body of Christ, we are all ministers, we are all a part of the "royal priesthood" (1 Pet 2:9). Together we are to win people to Christ and help them grow. The church needs someone whose primary responsibility is to preach the Word of God in such a way that the lost are saved and the Christians are motivated to use their gifts for the building up of the church. The minister should be allowed to focus on his areas of giftedness and to delegate responsibility.

> We are all the body of Christ, we are all ministers, we are all a part of the "royal priesthood."

The Minister's Responsibility

In this passage Paul mentions a threefold responsibility of the minister.

Teach

"These, then, are the things you should teach," Paul said. In a similar passage he admonished Timothy, "Preach the Word; be prepared in season and out of season; correct, rebuke and encourage—with great patience and careful instruction" (2 Tim 4:2).

Harry Emerson Fosdick used to say that a minister should spend an hour in preparation for every minute in the pulpit. When you hear a sermon, you should learn something about the Bible. It doesn't have to be something brand new every time; maybe it will just be a refresher on some of the basics. But we should be students of the Word, ever learning the truth of God.

The Bible has tremendous power when it is taught. "For the word of God is living and active. Sharper than any double-edged sword, it penetrates even to dividing soul and spirit, joints and marrow; it judges the thoughts and attitudes of the heart" (Heb 4:12). That's why when I was preaching every week, I most enjoyed preaching through a book of the Bible. People would come up to me later and say, "Have you been talking to my children? Do you have a pipeline into our home? How did you know what we were dealing with?" When the Bible is taught, it penetrates the thoughts and attitudes of the heart.

But our teaching of the Bible should be more than just relaying facts. If you leave church and all you learned was the size of Noah's ark, that probably won't help you in your everyday life. The preacher needs to tell you both what the Bible says and how that applies to you. In his book *Between Two Worlds*, John Stott said it is the preacher's job to build a bridge between the biblical world and the modern world. Bob Shannon said, "I don't go into the pulpit to explain a passage; I go into the pulpit to meet a need. It just so happens that for every need, there is a passage. When you get the two together, preaching is powerful."

> It is the preacher's job to build a bridge between the biblical world and the modern world.

Encourage

Paul told Titus not only to teach but to "encourage" as well. It's easy to get discouraged in our world. You can get beat down in your job, the news is depressing, your health may not be that great, and your family may be falling apart. When you come to church, you need some hope.

The gospel of Jesus Christ is good news! Jesus said, "I have come that they may have life, and have it to the full" (John 10:10). The Scripture says, "For everything that was written in the past was written to teach us, so that through endurance and the encouragement of the Scriptures we might have hope" (Rom 15:4). You shouldn't always walk out of church feeling beat down. David said, "I was glad when they said unto me, Let us go into the house of the LORD" (Ps 122:1, KJV).

Jesus Christ is our model teacher. They called him Rabbi, "Good Teacher." He often encouraged the brokenhearted with his words, saying things like, "In this world you will have trouble. But take heart! I have overcome the world" (John 16:33).

I once watched a tennis teacher who was billed as the greatest instructor of children in the region. He was responsible for instilling in some of the most famous tennis players their love for the sport. I

Respect Your Ministers

watched as he stood on one side of the net with several dozen tennis balls. On the other side of the net was a little girl about seven years old.

As he tried to teach her to hit the ball, he was a chatterbox of constant encouragement. "OK, Christine, hold the racket like I taught you. That's good! That's great! That's beautiful! Keep it up." He started hitting balls toward her. "Oh, you're doing great!" he said. "I'm proud of you. You almost hit that one. Look at that! Keep trying! Way to go!" The little girl was just beaming. She started huffing and puffing from the hard work, but she couldn't get enough. He was teaching her to love playing tennis, and he knew she would respond better to encouragement than to chastisement.

The preacher's job is to give the congregation a love for the Bible, a love for our Lord, and a love for the Christian life. Like that little girl, most people respond better to encouragement than chastisement.

Rebuke

Yet Paul reminded Titus that the minister also has a responsibility to "rebuke." Jesus said, "Those whom I love I rebuke and discipline" (Rev 3:19). Have you ever known someone who did nothing but flatter you all the time? "You look terrific," they say, no matter how bad you really look. You could be leaving the hospital and they would still say, "You look terrific." Eventually what they say doesn't matter to you anymore. They have to tell you the truth for the praise to be worthwhile. We should encourage whenever possible, but the minister who always praises and never rebukes will soon be tuned out.

> Most people respond better to encouragement than chastisement, but the minister who never rebukes will soon be tuned out.

On the other extreme are those who do nothing but rebuke. When I was in high school we had a preacher who was a rebuking specialist. He was a hellfire and brimstone machine. Every Sunday he would shout and holler and lay us low. For the first couple of sermons, we thought, *This guy is great. He tells it like it is. He convicts you.* But after two months we started wondering how long he was going to be around. We got tired of walking out each week with our tails between our legs. A loving person rebukes rarely, only when necessary, and does it honestly in order to motivate change.

Dr. Lewis Foster was a professor of mine in Bible college. Everybody respected him for his intelligence. He was a great teacher. He hardly ever rebuked, but one day in Bible survey class he looked down and saw two students in the second row playing tic-tac-toe. He stopped his lecture and stared at them but they didn't notice. They just kept playing! The rest of us felt the hairs on the back of our necks standing up from fear. He walked over and stood beside them. Suddenly they looked up, and there was the professor staring down at them!

He said inquisitively, "Who's winning?"

The only sound you could hear was the whir of the ceiling fan. He stared down at the tic-tac-toe game for about 15 eternal seconds. Then he walked back up to the platform, picked up his notes, and started lecturing again. Nobody ever played tic-tac-toe in his class again!

Jesus is our model, and he could rebuke harshly when it was necessary. He could say, "You scribes and Pharisees, hypocrites! You're like whitewashed tombs, clean on the outside, but inside you're full of dead men's bones." But Jesus could also rebuke gently. When Simon Peter denied him, Jesus simply turned and looked at Peter, and Peter was convicted. The most effective rebukes are not harsh, loud, or condemning. They can be spoken quietly and gently. But the rebuker motivates the "rebukee" to change.

> The most effective rebukes can be spoken quietly and gently, but the rebuker motivates change.

The Minister's Authority

Titus is told to teach, encourage, and rebuke "with authority." Where does the minister get his authority? Paul said, "Don't let anyone despise you." What right does a minister have to tell people what to do? I think the minister's authority is based on five sources.

The Call of God

God has anointed some people to teach and preach. If you sense that a person has been gifted in that way and is called by God to be a minister, respect that role.

The Word of God

A minister's opinions are no more binding on the believer than anyone else's, but if the minister is teaching the Bible, Christians should respect that as authoritative.

A Life of Integrity

There is great power in a good man who lives according to the Scriptures while moving among the people. But if he sacrifices that integrity, he will lose this source of authority.

A Life of Service

Jesus was a servant leader. He did not lead by intimidation but by example. He washed his disciples' feet, then he said,

> You know that the rulers of the Gentiles lord it over them, and their high officials exercise authority over them. Not so with you. Instead, whoever wants to become great among you must be your servant, and whoever wants to be first must be your slave—just as the Son of Man did not come to be served, but to serve, and to give his life as a ransom for many (Matt 25:28).

As we discussed earlier, the term *minister* means "servant," so our authority comes not from lording over others but trying to serve.

The Support of Church Leaders

God has designated a group of men called elders to be the overseers of the church. The elders are to direct the affairs of the church, and the minister's authority is only as good as the church leaders who stand behind him. Here's a leadership formula to remember:

Responsibility – Authority = Frustration

Responsibility minus authority equals frustration. If the church leaders undermine his credibility by being disrespectful or outright antagonistic, then the minister has no leverage and he is rendered ineffective. If they stand together in support of him, then he has authority. Just as a teacher has no authority in the classroom if the principal does not back her up, so the minister loses his authority if the board of elders doesn't stand behind him.

The minister loses his authority if the board of elders doesn't stand behind him.

The Church Member's Responsibility

The Bible commands us, "Obey your leaders and submit to their authority. They keep watch over you as men who must give an account. Obey them so that their work will be a joy, not a burden, for that would be of no advantage to you" (Heb 13:17). We are to obey and respect our ministers. Here are some practical suggestions on how you can show respect to your church leaders:

Be Submissive

I've been in church services where 75 people are sitting in the back of a church building that seats 300. Invariably, the preacher will get up and say, "During this first song, let's all move forward and sit near the front." Half of the congregation will move forward. The other half arrogantly folds their arms, as if to say, "Make me, preacher!" Unless it violates our convictions, we should have a submissive spirit and cooperate when we're asked to do something.

Be Studious

Don't automatically take everything the preacher says as gospel. Make sure you compare what he says with what the Bible says. Be like the Bereans. "Now the Bereans were of more noble character than the Thessalonians, for they received the message with great eagerness and examined the Scriptures every day to see if what Paul said was true" (Acts 17:11). A preacher who is honestly trying to preach the truth will appreciate the people who have their Bibles opened and are studying with him, because he knows the source of truth is God's Word, not himself.

Be Prayerful

It's been said that prayerless pews make powerless pulpits. Make a covenant to pray for one of your ministers every day. Pray that he will remain faithful in his personal life. Pray that he will seek God's will. Pray that he will be a good family man and that his family will be protected from harm and temptation. Pray that he will have the wisdom and energy to make good decisions and lead well. Your minister is leading people in a spiritual battle and he needs your prayers. The Bible says, "The prayer of a righteous man is powerful and effective" (Jas 5:16).

> Pray for one of your ministers every day.

Be Encouraging

Ministers take a lot of criticism, and they are typically very hard on themselves. A minister's work is never finished. You never feel like you studied long enough, prayed hard enough, visited enough people, shook enough hands, listened intently enough, smiled enough, or cared enough. With your words of encouragement you can keep your minister going in the right direction and inspired to continue ministering.

There's a story in Exodus 17 about a day that Israel battled the army of the Amalekites. Moses, the leader of God's people, didn't go into the battle. Instead he stood at the top of the hill and held out the staff of God. The Scripture reads,

> As long as Moses held up his hands, the Israelites were winning, but

whenever he lowered his hands, the Amalekites were winning. When Moses' hands grew tired, they took a stone and put it under him and he sat on it. Aaron and Hur held his hands up—one on one side, one on the other—so that his hands remained steady till sunset. So Joshua overcame the Amalekite army with the sword (Exod 17:11-13).

The task of God's people is the same today. There is an awesome spiritual battle going on. The ministers are to be God's leaders in the battle. As they go, so goes the church. When your minister's arms grow weary and his spirit grows weak, it is the congregation's task to undergird and support him, to hold him up, until the victory is won. 3:16

> When your minister's arms grow weary, it is the congregation's task to support him.

Promoting Growth through Respect for Ministers

1. Which has the greatest impact on you: when your minister teaches, encourages, or rebukes?

2. Name the three things you most appreciate about your minister.

3. Do you think your congregation does a good job respecting your ministers? How could you do better?

4. List five things you or your group could do to encourage your ministers. Would you do at least one of them this week?

Memory Verse Titus 2:15	*These, then, are the things you should teach. Encourage and rebuke with all authority. Do not let anyone despise you.*

CHAPTER NINE

EXPRESS A SWEET SPIRIT

TITUS 3:1-8

Many years ago I read a chapter in a book by Bruce Larson with a title I've never forgotten: "Are You Fun to Live With?" The more we grow to be like Jesus Christ, Larson said, the more other people ought to enjoy being around us. Jesus had a congenial spirit about him that attracted people. The more we grow to be like Christ, the more his disposition should be reflected in us. Christians should not be mean-spirited, quick-tempered, hypercritical people. We ought to be developing inside us a pleasantness that makes us easy to live with. If the church is to continue representing Jesus Christ to the world, there ought to be a sweet spirit about us.

In Titus 1:1-8, Paul instructs Titus to remind the people how and why they should represent Jesus with a sweet spirit.

Some Practical Ways to Express a Sweet Spirit

Remind the people to be subject to rulers and authorities, to be obedient, to be ready to do whatever is good, to slander no one, to be peaceable and considerate, and to show true humility toward all men (Titus 3:1,2).

Be Respectful of Authority

The Bible mentions four spheres of life where we as Christians should show respect to the ones in authority: the church, the home, the workplace, and the government. In other parts of this book we've discussed how employees should obey their employers, how Christians should respect their ministers and elders, and how wives should submit to their husbands. Here Paul mentions the importance of Christians showing honor to governing officials—the "rulers." Christians should be model citizens, respecting the government officials and obeying the laws.

Paul wrote about this principle in more detail to the Romans:

> Everyone must submit himself to the governing authorities, for there is no authority except that which God has established. The authorities that exist have been established by God. Consequently, he who rebels against the authority is rebelling against what God has instituted, and those who do so will bring judgment on themselves. For rulers hold no terror for those who do right, but for those who do wrong. Do you want to be free from fear of the one in authority? Then do what is right and he will commend you. For he is God's servant to do you good. But if you do wrong, be afraid, for he does not bear the sword for nothing. He is God's servant, an agent of wrath to bring punishment on the wrongdoer. Therefore, it is necessary to submit to the authorities, not only because of possible punishment but also because of conscience (Rom 13:1-5).

We should respect the government authorities even when they are imperfect. The church has a much greater impact in the community when its members are model citizens. Since our institutions are run by people, the institutions will be imperfect. But their source of authority is God, and we are to honor the position even when the person isn't honorable.

It's very common today for comedians and late night talk show hosts to belittle the President and show a complete disrespect for the man and the office. One Hollywood actor recently suggested that now that the President's daughters are old enough for the military, they should enlist and fight in Iraq or else they were huge hypocrites.

Contrast that common attitude with David's interactions with King Saul. The king was a madman; evidently he was bipolar. He was trying to kill David and was abusing his authority. David was hiding with his men in the deep recesses of a cave when King Saul, not knowing David was there, came to the mouth of the cave to rest. David's men whispered to him, "The Lord has delivered your adversary into your hand! Take his life and the throne will be yours!" David would have been justified. He tiptoed up to the king and cut off a piece of Saul's robe, but he didn't take the king's life.

When David returned to his men, they continued to urge him to kill the king. He told them he felt guilty even for cutting his robe and rebuked his men for wanting to kill Saul. "The Lord forbid that I should do such a thing to my master, the Lord's anointed, or lift my hand against him; for he is the anointed of the Lord" (1 Sam 24:6).

We should respect government officials for their position, even if their character is not perfect. That's hardest to do when the person in office is not the one for whom you voted. But Christians should set the tone by respecting even those with whom we disagree, "for there is no authority except that which God has established" (Rom 13:1).

> We should respect government officials for their position, even if their character is not perfect.

Guard against the sarcastic comments, mean-spirited and hateful accusations and belittling jokes that characterize the way most people refer to their governing officials. Although you may not agree with the decisions or lifestyles of certain leaders, don't humiliate them or ridicule them. When your children are in the presence of the mayor, the congressman, or the county judge, teach them to show respect. When someone from the opposite party is speaking on television, don't let your kids hear you making snide remarks. We shouldn't cower before government officials, because we answer to a higher, more powerful Authority. But we are called to respect them as if they are representatives of God.

We should also obey the law, even if it is unreasonable. Paul says not only to be subject to rulers, but to be "obedient" as well. Christians should be model citizens in obeying the laws, even when we aren't sure we agree with them. When the speed limit sign says "65 MPH," when the law says to pay a tax, when the code says don't build without a permit, Christians should do their best to obey the laws.

In certain situations where the government is disorganized that can be extremely difficult. I've heard missionaries complain that it is impossible to obey the laws in their country because they contradict one another. One law says your property must have a driveway; another says no driveways are permitted. No government official is willing to tell you which law is right. It takes a lot of discernment to know how to respect the government in such a situation and to follow the spirit of the law and the will of God.

But in America, we rarely have that problem. Usually we don't like the laws because they inconvenience us, not because they contradict each other. There will always be rules we don't like. Have a submissive spirit and obey anyway.

The only time we have the right to disobey the law is when obedience would force us to disobey God's commandments. If there is a man-made law that conflicts with God's instructions in the Bible, we are to disobey that law. When the apostles were told by the governing officials not to preach in the name of Jesus anymore they responded, "We must obey God rather than men!" (Acts 5:29).

We can complain about all the things that are wrong with our country, but we should be thankful for the freedoms God has granted and the wonderful blessings this country affords us. Christians living in America have no excuse. We among all people should have grateful hearts and submissive spirits.

Do Whatever Is Good

In addition to submitting to the government, Paul said, "Be ready to do whatever is good," (Titus 3:1). Jesus gave us this simple rule: "Do to others as you would have them do to you" (Luke 6:31). Expressing a sweet spirit doesn't just mean refraining from evil. It means looking for opportunities to do good to your neighbor.

John Bentley is an American lawyer who felt led of God to leave behind a comfortable lifestyle in the Pacific Northwest and establish an orphanage in China. John and his wife Lisa settled in Beijing and began accepting children who were considered beyond help by the government orphanages. They now minister to special needs children. Most of the children in their orphanage are missing limbs or have very serious physical problems.

I recently had the opportunity to meet John and Lisa and some of their children. One boy they named Levi was found abandoned in a field when he was just six weeks old. When he was first found, he was screaming in pain from burns that covered eighty percent of his body. A dollar and twenty five cents had been pinned to Levi's clothing with a note stating that the money was to help with the baby's burial. By God's grace and through the Bentleys' loving care, Levi survived and is now seven years old. He has only one arm, no hands or feet, and his body is severely scarred. But Levi's contagious smile and buoyant personality are a source of joy to the Bentleys and all who meet him.

As a result of John and Lisa doing good, John has gained a great deal of respect among the Chinese officials and in the local community, and the gospel of Christ has an increased credibility.

Do Not Slander

In his directives to Titus, Paul continued, "Remind the people to . . . slander no one" (Titus 2:1,2). Alice Roosevelt, the daughter of Teddy Roosevelt, was known for her caustic tongue. Her slogan was, "If you can't say anything good about someone, come sit by me." Some

Christians are like that. They want you to tell them all the gossip and slander so they can pass it on.

Paul told Titus that the Cretans were liars (Titus 1:12), but he wanted Christians on the island to be different. They were to be distinctive. They were to practice the very un-Cretan activity of telling the truth and being kind to people.

Be Peaceable

"Be peaceable," Paul writes. Don't always be looking for a fight. Don't love to quarrel. Don't be threatening to sue your neighbor every time you get a chance. Don't go out of your way to make enemies. "If it is possible, as far as it depends on you, live at peace with everyone" (Rom 12:18). It's not always possible. There will always be some people you can't live with, or some things you can't sit by and watch without protest. But don't be the source of conflict. Make every effort to live in harmony with those around you. Sometimes we have to stand for what is right, but for the most part we make a greater impact when we are peaceable than when we picket.

> You can't always live at peace, but don't be the source of conflict.

Be Considerate

"Be considerate." Put the other person's feelings ahead of your own. In our country everybody feels obligated to stand up for his rights. The Christian should look for opportunities to relinquish his rights, to be submissive, and to serve others. What a contrast to the ACLU and the spirit of our day!

Be Humble

Paul concludes this list by saying, ". . . show true humility toward all men" (Titus 2:2). The Revised Standard Version translates this phrase, "Show perfect courtesy towards all men." Don't bully people. Don't strut like you're superior. Treat people with courtesy. Note that important phrase, "toward all men." Be courteous not just towards those who can reciprocate or those who are on the same socioeconomic level as you. "Toward all men" means you treat the waitress with the same kindness that you do the owner of the restaurant. You are as polite to the cab driver as you are to the airline pilot. You are as kind to the janitor as to the principal.

Why We Should Express a Sweet Spirit

If you are not pleasant in spirit, it is because you have forgotten what God has done for you, or else you haven't really allowed him to transform you. Once we understand who we are in Jesus Christ, we can't help but have a new disposition. In the next section of Titus, Paul reminds us what we once were and what God did for us.

> Once we understand who we are, we can't help but have a new disposition.

What We Once Were

Paul begins by reminding us what we once were without Christ: "At one time we too were foolish, disobedient, deceived and enslaved by all kinds of passions and pleasures. We lived in malice and envy, being hated and hating one another" (Titus 3:3).

We were foolish. The Bible defines a fool as someone who says there is no God (Ps 14:1). A man doesn't have to be an atheist to be a fool. A fool is just someone who doesn't honor God, who refuses to acknowledge God's authority over his life. A man can be brilliant, wealthy, and influential, but if he doesn't honor God, he is a fool. Jesus said, "What good will it be for a man if he gains the whole world, yet forfeits his soul?" (Matt 16:26). Before we submitted to Christ, we foolishly acted as if God didn't matter.

We were disobedient to God. In our pride we were determined to prove that we were self-sufficient. We defied God's instructions about putting others ahead of ourselves, being generous with our money, living a pure life, and abiding by God's moral standards.

We were deceived. If a man is wrong about God and his Word, then that man is vulnerable to all kinds of false philosophies. The Bible says, "There is a way that seems right to a man, but in the end it leads to death" (Prov 14:12). The enemy of our souls is feeding us with all kinds of deceptive ideas that will destroy us in the end. Before you came to Christ, you probably believed his lies. "If you want to be excited and happy, then have an affair," he whispered. "Go ahead and buy what you want; a little debt never hurt anyone." "You need a little alcohol to calm you down; you're a more pleasant person to be around when you've had a little bit to drink." "You've got to step on a few people to get to the top; they'll get over it." Following Satan's lies made you miserable and unhappy, and it hurt a lot of other people.

We were enslaved by all types of passions and pleasures. Sin is fun at first. But eventually the fun wears off and you realize you've been enslaved. There is a law of increased appetite and diminishing returns with sinful passions and pleasures. Even the language we use expresses this reality. We talk about someone being *entangled* in an affair, *consumed* by greed, or *addicted* to drugs.

The Bible says, "Don't you know that when you offer yourselves to someone to obey him as slaves, you are slaves to the one whom you obey—whether you are slaves to sin, which leads to death, or to obedience, which leads to righteousness?" (Rom 6:16). Stuart Briscoe wrote,

> If pleasure is the watchword of our lives, we can only be happy when we're having a pleasurable experience. Then we must never be bored and never engage in anything mundane or routine. . . . We spend all our time, money and energy trying to avoid the real world and we become enslaved by the desire to escape reality.

We were full of malice and envy, being hated and hating one another. *Malice* is seething anger looking to get even. *Envy* is resentment of what another person has to the point that you delight in his misfortune. When you are disobedient toward God and enslaved by your passions, your relationships suffer. It takes very little for you to get angry with someone or envious toward those who have what you don't have. Since you are not motivated to forgive, hatred builds up. When you act out in hatred toward someone, he usually retaliates. Then you hate him even more and you retaliate, and you create a vicious cycle. People hate you and you hate them.

Paul says "at one time we too were. . . ." He's not describing other people. Paul himself was a fool. He rejected Jesus Christ, was full of selfish ambition, was enslaved by his own passions, and seethed with hatred toward the church. He wasn't very pleasant to be around before Jesus Christ got hold of his life!

What God Did

> But when the kindness and love of God our Savior appeared, he saved us, not because of righteous things we had done, but because of his mercy. He saved us through the washing of rebirth and renewal by the Holy Spirit, whom he poured out on us generously through Jesus Christ our Savior, so that, having been justified by his grace, we might become heirs having the hope of eternal life (Titus 3:4-7).

God showed kindness to us though we had been unkind to him. God had the right to say, "I am the Creator of your souls. I am the one who made you. If you rebel against Me, I will wipe you off the face of the earth." Instead, he broke the cycle of hatred and responded with mercy and kindness. "At just the right time, when we were still powerless, Christ died for the ungodly" (Rom 5:6).

> God broke the cycle of hatred and responded with mercy and kindness.

Donald Barnhouse told of a fire that swept over his dad's prairie farm. Afterward his dad was walking across the farm and found a lump of charcoal that he thought was a stump. When he kicked it, several baby chicks came running out from beneath it. The lump was the remains of a mother hen who had seen that her little chicks would not be able to escape the sweeping flames. She had gathered them under her wings and had endured the fire so that her chicks might live.

That was Christ's response to us. Knowing that we would be engulfed and destroyed by the sin that so easily entangles us, he voluntarily remained on the cross, absorbing all the fiery blows of the evil one that we might live.

In these verses Paul highlights three benefits to Jesus' death on the cross:

God saved us. Jesus "saved us through the washing of rebirth" (v. 5). When someone is saved from something, it usually means he escaped some danger—he was saved from an embarrassing moment, from financial disaster, from drowning. The Bible says Christians are saved from the wrath of God, from the ominous consequences of our sin.

God gave us the Holy Spirit. In the first gospel sermon ever preached, Peter said to the people in Jerusalem, "You have crucified the Son of God." The people believed him. "What should we do," they asked? Peter responded, "Repent and be baptized, every one of you, in the name of Jesus Christ for the forgiveness of your sins. And you will receive the gift of the Holy Spirit" (Acts 2:38).

I hear people say, "I haven't become a Christian because I'm not sure I can live that life. I don't want to be a hypocrite." If you wait till you have your life straightened out, you will never respond to Christ. When you surrender your life to Christ, you are saying, "Lord, I am sinful. I need You to cleanse me. I am weak. I need You to empower me through Your Holy Spirit." Then God cleanses your heart of sin and fills it with the indwelling of the Holy Spirit. Paul said God's Spirit has been "poured out on us generously" (v. 6). Through the Holy Spirit you have increasing power to live the Christian life—power to overcome temptation, to testify about your faith, to understand Scripture, to witness to other people, to love the unlovely.

God gave us the promise of eternal life. Paul continued, ". . . so that, having been justified by his grace, we might become heirs having

Express a Sweet Spirit 9

the hope of eternal life" (v. 7). God promises that those who surrender to Christ will live forever in heaven even after we die. That's not just wishful thinking or something we say at a funeral to make everybody feel better. It is a fact based on the death and resurrection of Jesus Christ. He said, "I am the resurrection and the life. He who believes in me will live, even though he dies; and whoever lives and believes in me will never die" (John 11:25,26).

Think about how incredibly kind God has been to us. We were foolish and rebellious, but instead of punishing us, God came to us and saved us through the death of Jesus Christ on the cross. Then he gives us the Holy Spirit to empower us and promises to take us to live with Him in heaven when we die. Max Lucado says, "Grace is absurd to the human mind. In fact, the only thing more absurd than the gift is our stubborn unwillingness to receive it."

> **How incredibly kind God has been to us!**

With all that God has done for us, how can we not receive his grace and pass that grace on to others with a sweet spirit? Paul concludes this section of Titus by saying, "This is a trustworthy saying. And I want you to stress these things, so that those who have trusted in God may be careful to devote themselves to doing what is good. These things are excellent and profitable for everyone."

If the people of God devote themselves to doing what is good with a sweet spirit, it will be excellent and profitable not only for the church but for our nation and our world.

George Washington, upon his retirement from public life, wrote a letter to the governors of the 13 colonies. He concluded the letter,

> I now make it my earnest prayer, that God would have you, and the State over which you preside, in his holy protection, that he would incline the hearts of the Citizens to cultivate a spirit of subordination and obedience to Government, to entertain a brotherly affection and love for one another, for their fellow Citizens of the United States at large, and particularly for their brethren who have served in the Field, and finally, that he would most graciously be pleased to dispose us all, to do Justice, to love mercy, and to demean ourselves with that Charity, humility and pacific temper of mind, which were the Characteristicks of the Divine Author of our blessed Religion, and without an humble imitation of whose example in these things, we can never hope to be a happy Nation. ⬚

Promoting Growth with a Sweet Spirit

1. There are about six things we are commanded to do in the first two verses of Titus 3. Which of those six is the most difficult for you? How does it affect the body of Christ and your witness when you disobey that command? How can you change?

2. Talk about a person you have seen transformed by the power of the Holy Spirit. How quickly did he or she change? From your vantage point, what percentage of the person's change was "will power" and what percentage was the Holy Spirit's power?

3. In this chapter we reviewed the four spheres of authority under which we find ourselves: government, church, family, and work. Which of the four is the most difficult for you to submit to? What would help change your attitude?

4. Think of something good you or your group could do to encourage a local government official or a neighbor. Would you do it this week?

Memory Verse
Titus 3:1,2

Remind the people to be subject to rulers and authorities, to be obedient, to be ready to do whatever is good, to slander no one, to be peaceable and considerate, and to show true humility toward all men.

CHAPTER TEN

MAINTAIN
HARMONY

TITUS 3:9-15

My sons used to argue a lot. I guess that's normal among children, but it bothered me that they didn't get along. One of my lowest days as a father was the day I heard my two teenage boys shouting and banging around in a room upstairs and had to rush up to break up a nasty fist fight. I know you can't *imagine* such a thing happening in a preacher's home! I was disappointed in my sons. Why couldn't they learn to get along?

Our Heavenly Father feels much the same way about us. It grieves the heart of God when his people bicker and fight. Proverbs says that one of the seven things God hates is "a man who stirs up dissension among brothers" (Prov 6:16-19). Conversely, God is thrilled to see brothers and sisters in his family who have harmonious relationships. "How good and pleasant it is when brothers live together in unity!" (Ps 133:1).

> **God is thrilled to see members of his family have harmonious relationships.**

Jesus said, "By this all men will know that you are my disciples, if you love one another" (John 13:35). In his final prayer in the garden of Gethsemane, after Jesus prayed for his disciples, he turned his attention to us, saying,

> My prayer is not for them alone. I pray also for those who will believe in me through their message, that all of them may be one, Father, just as you are in me and I am in you. May they also be in us so that the

world may believe that you have sent me. I have given them the glory that you gave me, that they may be one as we are one: I in them and you in me. May they be brought to complete unity to let the world know that you sent me and have loved them even as you have loved me (John 17:20-23).

Many of the New Testament letters appeal to the churches to refrain from division and live in harmony. "Let us therefore make every effort to do what leads to peace and to mutual edification" (Rom 14:19). "I appeal to you, brothers, in the name of our Lord Jesus Christ, that all of you agree with one another so that there may be no divisions among you and that you may be perfectly united in mind and thought" (1 Cor 1:10). "Make every effort to keep the unity of the Spirit through the bond of peace" (Eph 4:3).

> **When churches bicker, it saps our energy, quenches our spirit, and negates our testimony.**

It is a serious matter to create discord in the family of God. When churches bicker, it saps our energy, quenches our spirit, and negates our testimony.

One of the reasons Southeast Christian Church has grown to be a large church over the last four decades is that there has never been a church split. From the beginning there has been a spirit of harmony in our fellowship, especially among the leaders. When something has threatened that union, people have been mature and have risen above it.

If you have ever been to a fighting church, you don't want to go back. I once met a man whose church was so battered by division that they had seen three preachers come and go in three years. He said to me, "I noticed on your church letterhead a slogan, 'Speaking the truth in love.' We don't have a slogan at our church but if we did it would be, 'If you want to fight, go to First Christian.'" That is sad!

Paul concludes his letter to Titus by stressing the importance of maintaining harmony in the church. His final emphasis is on unity among the brothers, one of the most important principles for a church to heed if it is to continue to honor God and expand its influence.

Avoid Controversy If Possible

"But avoid foolish controversies and genealogies and arguments and quarrels about the law, because these are unprofitable and useless" (Titus 3:9). Paul says to avoid *foolish* controversies. Not all controversy is foolish; some issues are critical and have to be discussed. But we should avoid stupid arguments and useless quarrels.

Many of the Jewish rabbis of Paul's day loved to invent things about which to argue. Some of them would spend time building up imaginary genealogies for the people of the Old Testament and then arguing about them. Others would spend endless hours discussing what could be done on the Sabbath day or which foods should be considered kosher.

We're not much different. People think they are spiritual if they can eloquently argue about the Bible. It's one thing to be able to discuss theology; it's another thing to be able to show kindness at home or be diligent at work. People can get so hung up on the tiny letters of the law that they miss the big picture.

> **People can get so hung up on the tiny letters of the law that they miss the big picture.**

Former Governor of Kentucky John Y. Brown once suffered a heart attack while he was in Florida. He drove himself to the hospital and told the nurse at the station, "I think I'm having a heart attack."

"Sir, your car is illegally parked," she barked. "You'll have to move it."

He said, "I'm really having chest pains."

She said, "Before you check in, you must move your car."

He said, "Ma'am, I'm John Y. Brown—the former Governor of Kentucky. I think I'm having a heart attack."

"Sir," she said, "Move your car and then we'll talk to you."

He went out and moved his car, then finally was allowed to check in.

It's easy to become a legalist and miss the more important task of caring for people. We have to constantly beware of this danger in the church. Some controversies in Christian circles have no solution. They take up endless hours in unproductive effort. We would be better off just not broaching the subject if it is going to create such controversy. People spend hours debating premillennial and amillennial views of the return of Jesus. Sunday school classes can spend weeks analyzing whether the world was created in six 24-hour days or a long span of time in six different segments. Churches can get stymied by whether the place they meet should be called the auditorium or the sanctuary, or whether the preacher should be called the pastor or the evangelist.

‡ Reasons to Avoid Foolish Controversies

In this text we can infer a couple of reasons to avoid foolish controversies.

They accomplish nothing. Paul calls them "unprofitable and useless." When you are finished arguing, your time has been wasted. What virtue is there in having a deep theological discussion that has been rehashed dozens of times when the simple tasks of the Christian life go undone?

In 1917, when the Russian revolution was rocking the streets of Petrograd, leaders of the Russian Orthodox Church were in a conference just blocks away from the fighting. They were having a heated debate about what color robes the priests should wear. We can spend lots of time on trivia when there is a revolution going on in the world. Paul told Titus to spend his time on the real issues and avoid useless, trivial controversies.

They are potentially divisive. The word for argument in Titus 3:9 is translated "strife" in other passages. What often begins as a discussion among friends quickly becomes strife. People get their egos involved and lose perspective. The argument escalates and causes division. I once read about a man who shot and killed another man over a difference of interpretation of the Bible.

> People get their egos involved and lose perspective.

In an editorial in the *Christian Standard*, Sam Stone wrote,

> Some years ago, I talked to a student from a small town where I preached. They had two congregations there, neither running more than 30 people. I asked her how there happened to be a second church in that town. Was it started because of some doctrinal question, or was it because of a personality difference?
>
> "Oh, it was doctrinal," she explained quickly. "The other group believed in having fellowship dinners."

Ways to Avoid Foolish Controversies

A first grade boy wrote the following essay about straight pins: "Pins are wonderful. They save thousands of lives every year."

His teacher said, "How do pins save thousands of lives?"

He said, "By not swallowing them."

Prevention is the best cure. Here are five ways to avoid controversy.

Change the subject. When you feel a discussion is moving toward controversy, make a right turn in the conversation and skillfully get out of it.

Don't bring it up. If you know it is a volatile subject, don't mention it. Thirty years ago my parents and I had a heated discussion about divorce and remarriage. We never fought about it again. I never brought it up, and neither did they. But we maintained a good relationship throughout our adult years partly because we knew which subjects to avoid.

Walk away. Sometimes because someone is forcing the issue, you don't have a choice. Walk away from the subject or walk away from the person if necessary, but don't fight.

Use your sense of humor. Solomon said, "A cheerful heart is good medicine" (Prov 17:22). One preacher, when asked his view on the second coming of Christ, said, "I don't know. I'm not on the programming committee, I'm on the welcoming committee." A good sense of humor can diffuse a lot of tense moments.

If necessary, avoid the person altogether. You may meet someone who is so primed for an argument that nothing else works. Paul suggests here that you "have nothing to do" with a divisive person (Titus 3:10). If you know someone who is always in the middle of controversy, always fighting about something, avoid him or her. "Bad company corrupts good character" (1 Cor 15:33). Say a polite "hello" and keep walking.

Confront Divisive People When Necessary

"Warn a divisive person once, and then warn him a second time. After that, have nothing to do with him. You may be sure that such a man is warped and sinful; he is self-condemned" (Titus 3:10,11). Paul told the Romans, "If it is possible, as far as it depends on you, live at peace with everyone" (Rom 12:18). But he also said, "When Peter came to Antioch, I opposed him to his face, because he was clearly in the wrong" (Gal 2:11). As much as possible, live at peace, but sometimes you have to confront someone to his face.

Categories of Divisive People

Notice it is the *divisive* person who has to be warned. Someone who is threatening the harmony of the church needs to be confronted, not someone who disagrees with you or is blocking your program. Three kinds of people can cause serious division in the church and must be confronted.

The False Teacher. Earlier in his letter, Paul told Titus to silence those who were "ruining whole households by teaching things they ought not to teach" (Titus 1:11). If a small group leader or Sunday school teacher began saying there was nothing wrong with people living together before they got married, or that a person must speak in tongues in order to have the Holy Spirit, or that he has determined the exact date of Christ's return, that teacher should be confronted because false teaching is potentially divisive.

The Immoral Example. When someone flagrantly flaunts immoral behavior in the church and refuses to repent, it can cause a lot of division. Paul chastised the leaders of Corinth for not confronting a man in their church who was living in incest. "Don't you know that a little yeast works through the whole batch of dough?" he said (1 Cor 5:6). If there is a flagrantly immoral situation in the church, the whole congregation will be negatively affected. It has to be confronted.

> If there is a flagrantly immoral situation in the church, the whole congregation will be negatively affected.

The Contentious Spirit. This third kind of divisive person is more subtle and perhaps more dangerous. Some people have an antagonistic spirit and are always stirring up dissension. Maybe it's by *gossip*; if you can almost always trace the rumors back to the same source, you have found the contentious spirit. Perhaps it's by *criticism*; they sit back on the sidelines, mumbling and ridiculing what is happening. Maybe they stir up trouble by *anonymous letters*; he doesn't have the courage to confront personally or the self-confidence to discuss the matter openly, so he writes a note without signing his name. Sometimes the contentious spirit can divide by *open rebellion*, saying things like, "If you don't do it my way, I will withdraw my financial support." (Credible leaders never buckle under ultimatums.)

Many people divide the church by their *hypersensitivity*. They make it known that their feelings get hurt easily, so people are always walking on eggshells around them. "Aunt Mabel would really be hurt if we dropped the Doxology from the order of service because her great-grandfather started this church and we have always sung the Doxology." Or, "Dorothy has sung in the pageant for four years straight. If she's not asked to sing again this year, it will hurt her feelings." It is amazing how much damage can be done to churches and small groups by people who seem quiet and unassuming but who regularly hold everyone hostage by the threat of a long-term pout.

How to Confront a Divisive Person

Jesus gave us a great pattern for confronting people who have wronged us, including those who may cause division in the church. He said,

> If your brother sins against you, go and show him his fault, just between the two of you. If he listens to you, you have won your brother over. But if he will not listen, take one or two others along, so that "every matter may be established by the testimony of two or three witnesses." If he refuses to listen to them, tell it to the church; and if he refuses to listen even to the church, treat him as you would a pagan or a tax collector (Matt 18:15-17).

Here are some steps a church can take whenever we are faced with a potentially divisive situation.

Determine if the problem is measles or cancer. Every leader gets criticized occasionally. Sometimes you deserve it! Even if it is undeserved, not every critical comment or disagreement is going to result in division in the church. A healthy church is full of people who occasionally disagree but are able to do it maturely. When a serious issue arises, the leaders need to prayerfully discern whether the situation is more like measles or more like cancer. Measles may be uncomfortable but will quickly go away if left alone. Cancer won't disappear without aggressive treatment. If the situation isn't life-threatening, leave it alone. If it is potentially cancerous, confront it directly.

> A healthy church is full of people who occasionally disagree but are able to do it maturely.

Confront personally. Jesus said, "Go and show him his fault, just between the two of you." If you are the member of a small group where the leader is teaching false doctrine, or if someone in your circle of fellowship is gossiping in a way that could be divisive, you first go yourself to that person and plainly speak to him or her about your concern. That takes courage, but if the person repents, you have "won your brother over" without causing undue suffering.

Take two or three witnesses. If the person refuses to change, before taking it to the church, Jesus said to take two or three witnesses with you. You are still attempting to convince the divisive person privately that there is a problem. If no one will agree to go with you, perhaps the problem is not as serious as you are making it and you should drop it.

Discuss the problem with the church leaders. If, after taking the steps outlined above, you are still convinced he or she poses a threat to the harmony of the church, you should express your concern to the leaders of the church and trust them to deal with it properly. If they treat the matter as measles when you think it's cancerous, trust God, submit to your leaders, and let it go. It is not your job to be the church's vigilante. You have done your part.

The church leaders should warn the divisive person. Paul told Titus, "Warn a divisive person once, and then warn him a second time. After that, have nothing to do with him" (Titus 3:10). Keep in mind that Titus was a leader of the church. It is not the task of a church member to warn the divisive person, but of the leaders. "Brothers, if someone is caught in a sin, you who are spiritual should restore him gently" (Gal 6:1). This official warning should be done by the church leaders privately and in love.

I can recall an occasion early in my ministry when the wife of a deacon was threatening the harmony of the church with her constant murmuring and grumbling behind the scenes. She was what

Paul called a busybody and was creating unrest. Rather than just let it slide, the chairman of the elders approached her husband. The husband was a church officer, and it didn't seem right to confront his wife without his knowledge. The chairman said to him, "The elders are concerned about a problem in the church. Your wife is criticizing the vision of the church which the elders and the preacher have determined is God's will. Her criticism is divisive and is hurting the church. It needs to stop. What do you suggest we do?" Thankfully in this case, the deacon was a good and courageous man. He said humbly, "I'll see to it that it stops." It did.

The church should warn him a second time. Paul said that if there is no repentance and the body of Christ is still being threatened, the person should receive a second warning. This second confrontation from the church leaders should be more severe and involve a higher number of leaders.

If there is still no repentance, the church should discipline the divisive person. "After that, have nothing to do with him," Paul said. Jesus said, ". . . and if he refuses to listen even to the church, treat him as you would a pagan or a tax collector." In an extreme case, a person who refuses to repent after two warnings should be told by the elders that he or she is no longer a member of your congregation. You can still speak to him and be kind to him as you would a "pagan or a tax collector," but you don't treat him as a member of your fellowship. You don't give him leadership roles or recruit him for service opportunities.

I can remember only a few occasions when our church discipline reached the stage of dismissal. One involved a deacon's wife who abruptly announced she was divorcing her husband. The next week she brought her new boyfriend to church. When she was approached about her flagrant disobedience to God's command against divorce and adultery, she announced confidently that the marriage was over, she loved this new man, and she wanted to win him to the Lord. The elders informed her that adultery was not a valid method of evangelism and pleaded with her to repent and return to her husband. When she refused their godly but consistent counsel, she was informed and the congregation notified that she was no longer considered a member of the church. That was difficult, and some objected to such tough love, but it was essential to preserve the distinctiveness of the church. In the long run it proved to be the right decision.

Church leaders get nervous about exercising church discipline. It is uncomfortable, and most of us would like to avoid awkward confrontations. And leaders understandably want to avoid the extreme characterizations of the past. We don't want to be associated with witch hunts, burnings at the stake, and scarlet letters. And in this age of constant threats of legal action, church leaders are sometimes afraid to get into a legal quagmire. But I agree with Stuart Briscoe's warning: "If proper discipline is not applied where appropriate, the result will be a marked decline in the spiritual nature of the church."

> Tough love is essential to preserve the distinctiveness of the church.

I can count on two hands the number of times in my 40 years at Southeast that our elders had to confront an individual about divisiveness in our congregation. I can count on one hand the times they had to confront more than once. Usually the first confrontation was redemptive. If you know that the harmony of the church is so important that your church leaders will confront you if you threaten to divide the body, you will be less likely to be divisive.

When a doctor takes a knife and cuts into somebody to remove a malignant tumor, it temporarily hurts, but it is allowed because it is for the health of the whole body. Church leaders who care enough to confront, warn, and on rare occasions practice discipline, may cause temporary pain, but the ultimate harmony and purity that results is well worth the discomfort of spiritual surgery.

Practice Servanthood at Every Opportunity

As soon as I send Artemas or Tychicus to you, do your best to come to me at Nicopolis, because I have decided to winter there. Do everything you can to help Zenas the lawyer and Apollos on their way and see that they have everything they need. Our people must learn to devote themselves to doing what is good, in order that they may provide for daily necessities and not live unproductive lives.

Everyone with me sends you greetings. Greet those who love us in the faith. Grace be with you all (Titus 3:12-15).

The best way to maintain harmony in the church is for the leaders and members alike to get their minds off themselves and onto serving and loving other people. William Barclay wrote,

Half the trouble that arises in the church concerns rights, privileges, places and prestige. Someone has not been given his or her place. Someone has not been thanked. Someone has been neglected. Someone has been given a more prominent place on the platform than somebody else and there is trouble.

Most of our divisions are personality-driven, not issue-driven. We often think we are fighting for principle when we are just defending our own ego. We are jealous that someone else is in the limelight instead of

Most of our divisions are personality-driven, not issue-driven.

us, or we're angry because someone hurt our feelings. But when we get our minds off of ourselves and onto serving other people, harmony develops.

There was bickering and division in the upper room on the night of the Last Supper. The disciples were fighting about who was the most important. They were so egotistical that none of them would dare stoop to wash the feet of the others. Jesus got a basin of water and a towel, washed their feet, and said, "Now that I, your Lord and Teacher, have washed your feet, you also should wash one another's feet" (John 13:14). There is hardly ever any bickering over the basin. Jesus said, "The greatest among you will be your servant" (Matt 23:11).

As you read the final phrases of Paul's letter to Titus, you can't help but notice the consideration the early Christians had for each other. Paul reminds Titus to pay attention to people's specific needs—even his own. "Do your best to come to me at Nicopolis. . . . Do everything you can to help Zenas the lawyer and Apollos on their way and see that they have everything they need." Titus was to lead the way in serving others. He was to show the church that he himself was not an arrogant prima donna, but someone who put others' needs ahead of his own. That kind of spirit among the leaders of the church creates harmony. When we get our minds off ourselves and onto other people, it does marvelous things to our relationships. We quit criticizing others, we "devote ourselves to doing what is good," and we become supportive of others.

My sons get along much better today. In fact, they are the closest of friends. They talk on the phone almost every day and do a lot of things together. There is one big difference in both of them: maturity. They are in their late 30s. Both of them are married, and they have given me a total of seven grandchildren. Their wives love each other and care for one another.

It's a joy to watch your children mature, to see them laugh and love and serve together when they used to bicker and fight. How much joy it must give the Father to see his children living in harmony. The Bible says,

Speaking the truth in love, we will in all things grow up into him who is the Head, that is, Christ. From him the whole body, joined and held together by every supporting ligament, grows and builds itself up in love, as each part does its work (Eph 4:15,16).

Promoting Growth
Because We Love One Another

1. What is the most common disagreement among people in your congregation? Is it possible for two Christians to disagree about this issue? Should the issue be avoided altogether or resolved?

2. Have you ever been divisive? Is there an issue you have refused to let die? Has your need to be right become more important than the more obvious commands to submit and love and maintain harmony? If so, make sure to repent and do your best to reconcile.

3. Of the three types of divisive people, which one are you most tempted to be? How can you avoid falling into Satan's trap and dividing the body of Christ?

4. Which are you less likely to do: Confront someone who is causing division, or take it to the next step if the confrontation doesn't work?

5. This book summarizes ten directives from God for you and your congregation. Which of the ten is the most difficult for you to follow? Which of the ten is the easiest? How can you improve in your area of difficulty?

6. Of the ten directives, which one does your church do the best? Take some time this week to encourage your elders and thank them for successfully following God's directive in this area.

Memory Verse
Titus 3:9,10

But avoid foolish controversies and genealogies and arguments and quarrels about the law, because these are unprofitable and useless. Warn a divisive person once, and then warn him a second time. After that, have nothing to do with him.

THE 3:16 SERIES

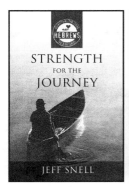

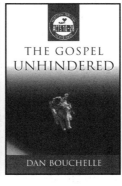

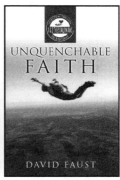

**Strength for
the Journey**
Hebrews
Jeff Snell
108 pgs, soft
GCAD-917-4, $7.99

**The Gospel
Unleashed**
Acts 1-9
Dan Bouchelle
108 pgs, soft
GCAD-493-8, $7.99

**The Gospel
Unhindered**
Acts 10-28
Dan Bouchelle
108 pgs, soft
GCAD-499-7, $7.99

**Unquenchable
Faith**
1&2 Thessalonians
David Faust
137 pgs, soft
GCAD-492-X, $7.99

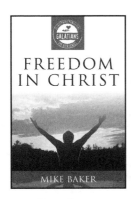

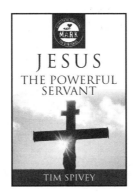

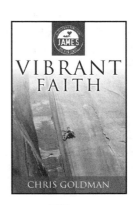

**Freedom
in Christ**
Galatians
Mike Baker
120 pgs, soft
GCAD-299-4, $7.99

**Jesus the
Powerful Servant**
Mark
Tim Spivey
108 pgs, soft
GCAD-945-X, $7.99

**Vibrant
Faith**
James
Chris Goldman
108 pgs, soft
GCAD-499-7, $7.99

Titus 2:1

You must teach what is in accord with sound doctrine.

Titus 1:8,9

Rather he must be hospitable, one who loves what is good, who is self-controlled, upright, holy and disciplined. He must hold firmly to the trustworthy message as it has been taught, so that he can encourage others by sound doctrine and refute those who oppose it.

Titus 1:15

To the pure, all things are pure, but to those who are corrupted and do not believe, nothing is pure. In fact, both their minds and consciences are corrupted.

Titus 2:7b,8

In your teaching show integrity, seriousness and soundness of speech that cannot be condemned, so that those who oppose you may be ashamed because they have nothing bad to say about us.

Titus 2:7a

In everything set them an example by doing what is good.

Titus 2:9,10

Teach slaves to be subject to their masters in everything, to try to please them, not to talk back to them, and not to steal from them, but to show that they can be fully trusted, so that in every way they will make the teaching about God our Savior attractive.

TITUS MEMORY VERSES

Titus 2:11,12

For the grace of God that brings salvation has appeared to all men. It teaches us to say "No" to ungodliness and worldly passions, and to live self-controlled, upright and godly lives in this present age.

Titus 2:15

These, then, are the things you should teach. Encourage and rebuke with all authority. Do not let anyone despise you.

Titus 3:1,2

Remind the people to be subject to rulers and authorities, to be obedient, to be ready to do whatever is good, to slander no one, to be peaceable and considerate, and to show true humility toward all men.

Titus 3:9,10

But avoid foolish controversies and genealogies and arguments and quarrels about the law, because these are unprofitable and useless. Warn a divisive person once, and then warn him a second time. After that, have nothing to do with him.

HEARTSPRING PUBLISHING